Adobe
Dimension
2020 release

CLASSROOM IN A BOOK®
The official training workbook from Adobe

Keith Gilbert

Executive Editor: Laura Norman
Development Editor: Susan Everson
Technical Reviewer: Pete Rivard
Senior Production Editor: Tracey Croom
Copyeditor: Susan Everson
Composition: Keith Gilbert
Proofreader: Becky Winter
Indexer: Valerie Haynes-Perry
Cover Illustration: Jesus Bibian Jr., behance.net/ChewyPixels
Cover Designer: Eddie Yuen
Interior Designer: Mimi Heft

ISBN-13: 978-0-13-658393-6

ISBN-10: 0-13-658393-8

WHERE ARE THE LESSON FILES?

Purchase of this Classroom in a Book in any format gives you access to the lesson files you'll need to complete the exercises in the book.

1 Go to www.adobepress.com/DimensionCIB2020.

2 Sign in or create a new account.

3 Click Submit.

Note: If you encounter problems registering your product or accessing the lesson files or web edition, go to www.adobepress.com/support for assistance.

4 Answer the questions as proof of purchase.

5 The lesson files can be accessed through the Registered Products tab on your Account page.

6 Click the Access Bonus Content link below the title of your product to proceed to the download page. Click the lesson file links to download them to your computer.

Note: If you purchased a digital product directly from www.adobepress.com or www.peachpit.com, your product will already be registered. However, you still need to follow the registration steps and answer the proof of purchase question before the Access Bonus Content link will appear under the product on your Registered Products tab..

CONTENTS

GETTING STARTED

Adobe Dimension gives designers the ability to quickly composite 3D and 2D elements in a scene, customize models, specify materials, and create realistic lighting. Once the final staged scene is assembled, the advanced rendering engine in Dimension will output the scene to a two-dimensional Photoshop file complete with realistic textures, materials, shadows, and reflections. Dimension is perfect for advertising, product design, scene visualization, abstract art, package design, or creative exploration.

About Classroom in a Book

Adobe Dimension Classroom in a Book (2020 release) is part of the official training series for Adobe graphics and publishing software, developed with the support of Adobe product experts. The lessons are designed to let you learn at your own pace. If you're new to Adobe Dimension, you'll learn the fundamental concepts and features that you'll need to master the program. And if you've been using Adobe Dimension for a while, you'll find that Classroom in a Book teaches many advanced features, including tips and techniques for using the latest version of the application and creating realistic scenes with 3D models.

Although each lesson provides step-by-step instructions for creating a specific project, there's room for exploration and experimentation. You can follow the book from start to finish or do only the lessons that match your interests and needs. Each lesson concludes with a review section summarizing what you've covered.

Prerequisites

Before you begin to use *Adobe Dimension Classroom in a Book (2020 release),* you should have a working knowledge of your computer and its operating system. Make sure that you know how to use the mouse and standard menus and commands, and also how to open, save, and close files. If you need to review these techniques, see the documentation for your Microsoft Windows PC or Apple Mac computer.

To complete the lessons in this book, you'll need to have Adobe Dimension installed. It will also be helpful to have Adobe Photoshop and Adobe Illustrator installed for exploration in a couple of the lessons.

Installing Adobe Dimension

Before you begin using *Adobe Dimension Classroom in a Book (2020 release)*, make sure that your system is set up correctly and that you've installed the required software. You must license the Adobe Dimension software separately. For system requirements and complete instructions on installing the software, visit helpx. adobe.com/dimension/system-requirements.html.

A couple of the lessons in this book use Adobe Photoshop and Adobe Illustrator. You can install Photoshop and Illustrator on your computer using the Adobe Creative Cloud desktop application, available at adobe.com/creativecloud/desktop-app.html. Follow the on-screen instructions.

Starting Adobe Dimension

You start Dimension just as you do most software applications.

To start Adobe Dimension in Mac: Click the Adobe Dimension icon in the Launchpad or Dock.

To start Adobe Dimension in Windows: Click the Start button in the taskbar, and in the alphabetical list under A, click Adobe Dimension.

If you don't see Adobe Dimension, type **Dimension** into the search box in Spotlight (Mac), in the taskbar (Windows), and when the Adobe Dimension application icon appears, select it and press Return/Enter.

Online content

Your purchase of this Classroom in a Book includes online materials provided by way of your Account page on adobepress.com. These include:

Lesson files

To work through the projects in this book, you will need to download the lesson files by following the instructions below.

Web Edition

The Web Edition is an online interactive version of the book providing an enhanced learning experience. Your Web Edition can be accessed from any device with a connection to the Internet and it contains:

- The complete text of the book
- Hours of instructional video keyed to the text
- Interactive quizzes

Accessing the lesson files and Web Edition

You must register your purchase on adobepress.com in order to access the online content:

1 Go to www.adobepress.com/DimensionCIB2020.

2 Sign in or create a new account.

3 Click Submit.

4 Answer the question as proof of purchase.

5 The lesson files can be accessed from the Registered Products tab on your Account page. Click the Access Bonus Content link below the title of your product to proceed to the download page. Click the lesson file link(s) to download them to your computer.

   The Web Edition can be accessed from the Digital Purchases tab on your Account page. Click the Launch link to access the product.

Note: If you encounter problems registering your product or accessing the lesson files or web edition, go to www.adobepress.com/support for assistance.

Note: If you purchased a digital product directly from www.adobepress.com or www.peachpit.com, your product will already be registered. However, you still need to follow the registration steps and answer the proof of purchase question before the Access Bonus Content link will appear under the product on your Registered Products tab.

Restoring default preferences

The preferences file stores information about various command settings in Dimension. Each time you quit Dimension, the selections you make in the Preferences dialog are saved in the preferences file.

To ensure that what you see on-screen matches the images and instructions in this book, you should restore the default preferences as you begin each lesson. If you prefer to preserve your preferences, be aware that the settings in Dimension may not match those described in this book.

To restore your preferences to the factory default, do the following:

1 Start Adobe Dimension.

2 Choose File > New to create a new, blank file.

3 Choose Adobe Dimension > Preferences (macOS) or Edit > Preferences (Windows).

4 Click Reset Preferences.

5 Click OK.

Additional resources

Adobe Dimension Classroom in a Book (2020 release) is not meant to replace documentation that comes with the program or to be a comprehensive reference for every feature. Only the commands and options used in the lessons are explained in this book. For comprehensive information about program features and tutorials, refer to these resources:

Adobe Dimension Learn and Support: helpx.adobe.com/support/dimension.html is where you can find and browse Learn and Support content on Adobe.com. You can go there directly from Dimension by choosing Help > Dimension Help.

Home screen: In Dimension, the Home screen contains various links to tutorials and other learning content.

Dimension tutorials: helpx.adobe.com/dimension/tutorials.html lists online tutorials for beginner and experienced users.

Getting Started with Adobe Dimension YouTube videos: In Dimension, choose Help > Learn.

Dimension blog: theblog.adobe.com/creative-cloud/dimension/ brings you tutorials, product news, and inspirational articles about Dimension.

Adobe Support Community: community.adobe.com lets you tap into peer-to-peer discussions, questions, and answers on Adobe products.

Adobe Dimension product home page: adobe.com/products/dimension.html provides information about product features and system requirements.

Resources for educators: adobe.com/education and edex.adobe.com offer a treasure trove of information for instructors who teach classes on Adobe software. Find solutions for education at all levels, including free curricula that use an integrated approach to teaching Adobe software and can be used to prepare for the Adobe Certified Associate exams.

Adobe Authorized Training Centers

Adobe Authorized Training Centers offer instructor-led courses and training on Adobe products.

A directory of AATCs is available at learning.adobe.com/partner-finder.html.

1 INTRODUCING ADOBE DIMENSION

Lesson overview

In this lesson, you'll explore the workspace and learn the following:

- What Adobe Dimension is.
- How to open a Dimension file.
- How to work with the tools and panels.
- How to change your view of a scene.
- How to make simple edits to a scene.

 This lesson will take about 45 minutes to complete. To get the lesson files used in this chapter, download them from the web page for this book at www.adobepress.com/DimensionCIB2020. For more information, see "Accessing the lesson files and Web Edition" in the Getting Started section at the beginning of this book.

The modern, uncluttered interface of Adobe Dimension makes it easy to find the tools and options you need.

Introducing Adobe Dimension

Adobe Dimension is a desktop program for Macintosh and Windows for creating photorealistic images from 3D assets for branding, product shots, scene visualization, and abstract art.

Dimension makes 3D design, compositing, and rendering accessible to people with little or no 3D software experience. Wherever possible, special terminology that is unique to the 3D modeling world is avoided in both the Dimension program and this book. The Dimension interface should be familiar to users of other Adobe design tools, such as Adobe XD, Illustrator, Photoshop, and InDesign.

Dimension is a subscription product, available as part of the Adobe Creative Cloud product offering. Depending on your subscription plan, you might be paying only for Dimension, or you might have access to all the Creative Cloud applications, including Adobe Photoshop and Illustrator, which are particularly useful as companions to Adobe Dimension.

Where do 3D models come from?

Dimension isn't intended for creating 3D models. 3D models are usually created with modeling software such as 3ds Max, Blender, Inventor, Maya, Rhino, Sketchup, SolidWorks, Strata 3D, and so on. Most of these products have a fairly steep learning curve, are quite technical, and, due to their complexity, aren't well-suited for part-time or occasional use.

Dimension's sweet spot is in importing models from these programs; it can then apply new materials to their surfaces, position them with other models, composite them into 2D scenes, and apply realistic lighting, reflections, and shadows. The result is then "rendered," or converted into a flat 2D image, as a PSD or PNG file that can be used in print publications or on websites or for other digital uses. Dimension also includes a feature that lets you export an interactive 3D version of the scene to a website to share with others.

1. Create a scene.

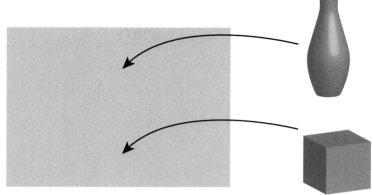

2. Adjust lighting, materials, size, position, rotation, etc.

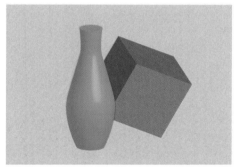

3. Add background.

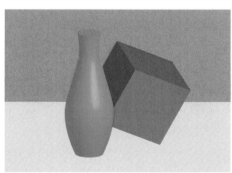

4. Output. Publish to Web. Render to PSD or PNG.

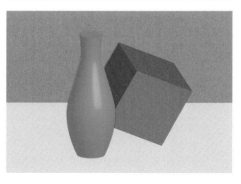

Starting Dimension and opening a file

In this lesson, you will open a finished Dimension scene and poke around a bit to learn how Dimension's interface is designed.

1 Launch Adobe Dimension.

The home screen is displayed. Your screen may look different than the screen capture shown here, and that's OK. The home screen contains links to various tutorials and other Dimension resources, as well as to any Dimension files you worked on recently.

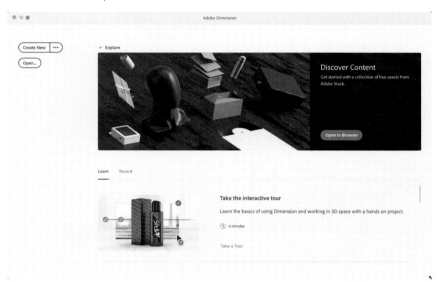

2 Click Open.

3 Select the file named Lesson_01_begin.dn, which is in the Lessons > Lesson01 folder that you copied onto your hard disk, and then click Open.

You'll use this simple 3D scene to explore the Dimension interface.

Dimension limitation: One file open at a time

3D files can be complex and demand a lot of computer memory and processing power. Because of this, Dimension allows you to open only a single file at a time. In other words, if you have a project open in Dimension and then create a new file or open another file, the file you originally had open will close.

Exploring the tools

The Tools panel on the far left side of the screen contains a handful of tools that you'll use to create and edit your 3D scenes. Let's take a tour of the Tools panel.

1   Hover over each of the tools in the Tools panel, and note that a blue tooltip is displayed. This tooltip tells you the name of the tool, the keyboard or mouse shortcut that can be used to access the tool, and what the tool is used for.

2   Note that the Tools panel is divided into sections by subtle horizontal lines.

The top tool—the Add And Import Content tool—is used to add content to your scene. Immediately below this is the Select tool. You'll use this tool more than any other, as it is used for selecting and transforming 3D models.

The next two tools—the Magic Wand and the Sampler—are grouped together because they are both used for selecting and changing the color or surface materials of just part of a larger 3D object, such as the cap on a bottle or the handle on a mug.

The next four tools—Orbit, Pan, Dolly, and Horizon—are used for adjusting the position of the "camera" in the 3D scene. These tools are often referred to as the camera tools.

The bottom two tools—the Zoom tool and the Hand tool—are used to adjust your view of the "canvas," or work area, on the screen. These tools work similarly to the Zoom and Hand tools in Photoshop, Illustrator, and InDesign.

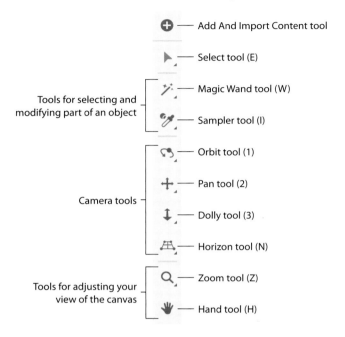

3 Right-click the Dolly tool, and note that some additional options for this tool appear on the screen.

The small black arrow in the lower-right corner of a tool in the Tools panel indicates that additional tools or tool options will appear if you right-click the tool, double-click the tool, or press and hold the mouse button on the tool.

Exploring the panels

As in many other Adobe design programs, panels on the right side of the screen display the properties of objects that you have selected in the work area; the panels allow you to edit those properties as well. Let's see how this works in Dimension.

1   Select the Select tool (keyboard shortcut: V) in the Tools panel.

2   Click the red chair in the scene. Note that the chair displays with a blue highlight to indicate that it is selected. A red, green, and blue Select tool widget is also displayed near the chair.

Explore the Scene panel

The Scene panel displays a list of all the components that make up the scene.

1   Look at the Scene panel on the right side of the screen. In this case, there are five objects in the scene: Environment, Camera, retro_green_chair, retro_table, and retro_red_chair.

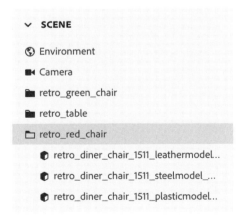

2 Right-click the Select tool in the Tools panel. In the tool options that appear, make sure that the Group Select option is turned on. This causes the tool to select the entire group when you click a grouped object, similar to the Selection tool in Photoshop, Illustrator, and InDesign.

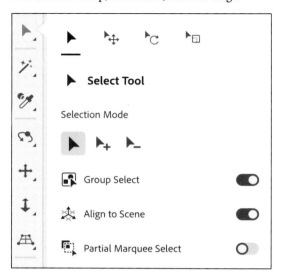

3 Click the green chair on the canvas (the "page" or the work area) to select it. This will highlight the retro_green_chair model in the Scene panel.

4 Hover over the retro_green_chair entry in the Scene panel, and you'll see an eye icon ⊙ to the right of the entry. Click this icon to hide the green chair on the canvas.

5 Click the eye icon again to show the model on the canvas.

6 Click the words "retro_table" in the Scene panel, and the table will be selected on the canvas. Sometimes selecting an entry in the Scene panel is an easier and more precise way to select a model than clicking the model on the canvas.

Explore the Actions panel

Depending on what you have selected in your scene, the Actions panel will display quick shortcuts to various "actions," or things that you can do to your selection.

1   With the retro_table model selected, the Actions panel displays the Delete, Duplicate, Group, and Move To Ground actions.

2   Hover over each action icon to see the name of the action as well as a keyboard shortcut that can be used for each.

Explore the Properties panel

Depending on what you have selected in your scene, the Properties panel displays various properties of the selection.

1   With the retro_table object selected, the Properties panel displays the "pivot" point, as well as X, Y, and Z values for Position, Rotation, and Scale, respectively. Each of these values can be edited.

2   Enter a value of **4 cm** in the X field for Position and press Return (macOS) or Enter (Windows). This will move the table to the right in the scene.

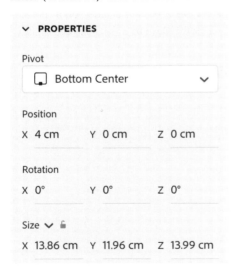

● **Note:** Unlike in some other Adobe products, these three panels (Scene, Actions, and Properties) cannot be removed or rearranged—they will always be displayed on the screen at the same location. You can collapse and expand each of these panels by clicking the disclosure arrow to the left of the panel name.

3   In the Scene panel, select Environment. The environment is the area around the 3D models that affects the lighting, reflections, and ground properties.

4   Below Environment in the Scene panel you'll see Environment Light and Sun displayed. Select Environment Light.

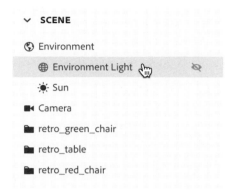

5   In the Properties panel, drag the Intensity slider to the left to about 75% to reduce the amount of overall light in the scene.

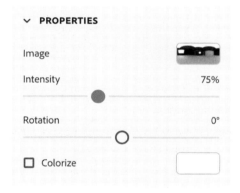

6   In the Scene panel, select Sun.

7   In the Properties panel, drag the Intensity slider to the right to about 175% to increase the strength of the sun light on the scene.

Understanding the Camera

Every Dimension project contains a single camera. You can manipulate the camera with the Orbit, Pan, Dolly, and Horizon tools to view the 3D scene from various angles, distances, and perspectives.

1   Select the Select tool in the Tools panel (keyboard shortcut: V).

2   Either select the red chair on the canvas or select the retro_red_chair object in the Scene panel.

3   In the Properties panel, enter **40°** for the Y value for Rotation, and press Return/ Enter. Note that the chair rotates around the vertical (y) axis.

4   Choose Edit > Undo Edit Scene to undo the rotation.

5   Choose Edit > Redo Edit Scene to redo the rotation.

Note that you just rotated an actual object (the red chair) within the scene. It's now oriented differently relative to the other objects in the scene.

6   Select the Dolly tool in the Tools panel (keyboard shortcut: 3). Drag down on the screen with your mouse to move the camera farther away from the object.

7   Choose Camera > Camera Undo to return to the original view of the object.

8   Select the Orbit tool in the Tools panel (keyboard shortcut: 1).

9 Drag around on the scene with the Orbit tool. This changes your view of the scene. It's as if you are flying around the scene, viewing the models from different angles through a camera lens.

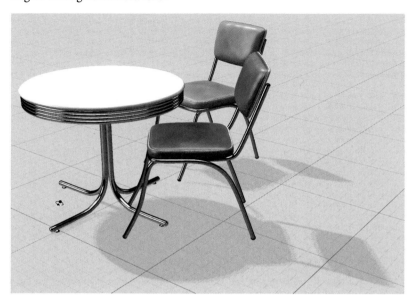

● **Note:** Dimension has two undo commands. Edit > Undo reverses the last actual edit that you made to the objects in your scene. Camera > Camera Undo reverses the last movement of the camera.

Note that as you rotate your view of the scene with the Orbit tool, you aren't changing the position of the objects in the scene relative to one another. Instead, you're simply changing the angle and distance from which you are viewing the models.

10 Choose Camera > Camera Undo as many times as necessary to return to the initial view of the scene.

Understanding the Canvas

So far, all our manipulation of our 3D scene has occurred inside a large rectangle that occupies most of your work area on the screen. This rectangle is called the "canvas." Think of the canvas as your "page." It's the actual dimensions of the final 2D image that is being created from your 3D objects. Most of the time, you'll probably just leave this canvas as it is on your screen, using the camera tools to change your view of the scene within the bounds of the canvas. Depending on what other software programs you may have used, it might be helpful to think of the canvas as the "viewport" into your 3D scene.

If you've used Adobe design tools such as Photoshop, Illustrator, or InDesign, you may want to manipulate your view of the canvas independently of the camera tools.

Tip: It might be helpful to think of the canvas this way: The camera tools (Orbit, Pan, Dolly, and Horizon) manipulate your view of the scene within the canvas. The Zoom and Hand tools manipulate your view of the canvas itself.

Tip: As with many other Adobe design tools, you can use the Command+plus and Command+minus (macOS) or Ctrl+plus and Ctrl+minus (Windows) keyboard shortcuts to zoom in and out. Use Command+1 (macOS) or Ctrl+1 (Windows) to see your design at 100%, and use Command+zero (macOS) or Ctrl+zero (Windows) to return to the "fit in window" view.

1   Select the Zoom tool in the Tools panel (keyboard shortcut: Z), and click the canvas or drag across the canvas to zoom in.

2   Select the Hand tool in the Tools panel (keyboard shortcut: H), and drag the scene to move the canvas around on the screen.

3   Select the Zoom tool in the Tools panel (keyboard shortcut: Z).

4   Hold down the Option key (Mac) or Alt key (Windows), and click the canvas a couple of times to zoom out.

5   Choose View > Zoom to Fit Canvas to fit the canvas on the screen.

Understanding the Ground Plane

The vanishing lines (the grid of squares that you see on the screen) represent the Ground Plane of the 3D scene. The ground plane is the "floor" that objects in the scene typically sit on, although objects can float above this floor or be buried below it.

1   Choose Camera > Switch To Home View to ensure that your camera view is back to the way it was at the beginning of this lesson.

2   Select the Select tool in the Tools panel (keyboard shortcut: V).

3   Select the retro_green_chair object in the Scene panel.

4   In the Properties panel, change the Z value for Rotation to **90°**, and press Return/ Enter. The chair rotates around the z-axis so that half of the chair disappears into the ground plane.

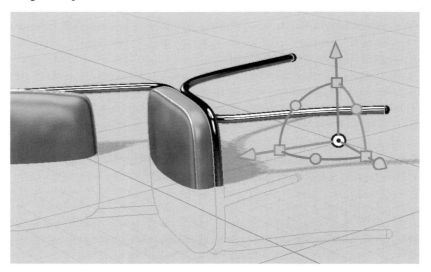

5   Choose Edit > Deselect All.

6   Select the Orbit tool in the Tools panel (keyboard shortcut: 1).

7   Drag down on the screen with the Orbit tool. This changes your view of the scene so that you are viewing it from above.

Note that the grid lines on the ground plane are dark gray and that the ground plane is opaque. In other words, you can't see through the floor to what is underneath.

8 Drag up on the screen with the Orbit tool until you can see the entire green chair. Now you are viewing the scene from below the ground plane, looking up at the bottom of the table.

Note that you can see both the part of the green chair that is sticking "up" from the ground and the part that is "buried" below the ground. When you are viewing the scene from below the ground plane, the ground plane appears transparent so that you can see through it to the objects above.

Note also that the grid lines on the underside of the ground plane are a reddish-gray color. This can help reduce confusion in those instances when you aren't sure if you are viewing a scene upside down or right-side up.

▶ **Tip:** The grid lines on the ground plane can be toggled on and off with View > Toggle Grid. And the ground plane itself can be turned on and off in the Properties panel when Environment is selected in the Scene panel.

9 Select the Dolly tool in the Tools panel (keyboard shortcut: 3). Drag down on the screen repeatedly with your mouse to move the camera farther away from the object. Note that the ground plane is "infinite." The camera can be moved a long way away from the object.

10 Choose Camera > Switch To Home View to return the camera view back to the way it was at the beginning of this lesson.

Using Render Preview

Getting an accurate view of the surfaces, colors, lighting, shadows, and reflections in a scene requires that a scene be rendered. Rendering is a processor-intensive, time-consuming task in which the computer analyzes how the objects in a scene interact with each other, the background, and the lighting in the scene, and then calculates accurate shadows, highlights, surface details, and reflections.

But even the fastest computers today are unable to render a complex scene in real time as you make edits to the scene. This is why rendering isn't usually done until the final stages of a project. However, the Render Preview feature gives you a quick, fairly accurate idea of what the final rendering will look like, almost in real time, as you work on a scene.

1 Click the Render Preview icon ▦ in the upper-right corner of the screen.

After a short delay (depending on the speed of your computer), you'll see a much more realistic scene on your screen. In particular, the lighting, shadows, and reflections will look much more realistic.

2 Select the Select tool in the Tools panel (keyboard shortcut: V).

3 Select the retro_green_chair in the Scene panel.

4 Drag the chair to the left. As you drag, you'll see that the render preview is temporarily disabled.

5 Choose Edit > Undo Transform to move the chair back where it was.

6   In the Properties panel, change the Z value for Rotation to **0°**, and press Return/
    Enter. After a brief delay, you'll see the Render Preview once again show you a
    realistic view of your scene.

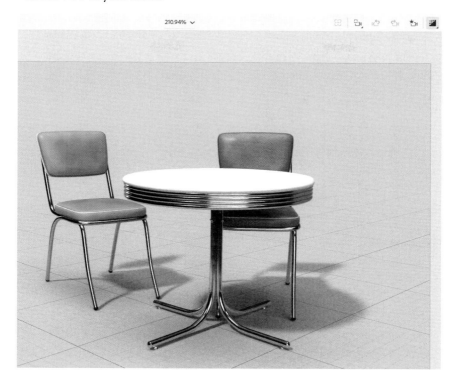

The two modes of Dimension

The Dimension interface consists of two modes: Design and Render. Design mode
is where you'll spend the lion's share of your time creating and editing 3D scenes.
Render mode is where you'll create the final, high-quality, pixel-perfect output of
your scene. You'll learn all about both of these modes throughout this book.

1   In the upper-left corner of the screen, you'll see a line underneath Design
    to indicate that you are currently in Design mode. Whenever you open a
    Dimension file or create a new file, Dimension will initially display the file
    in Design mode.

    Design   Render

2 Click Render to switch to Render mode. Note that the 3D content disappears from view and that all the tools and panels are replaced with new panels for controlling the render settings.

We'll cover the details of rendering in a later lesson. For now, I've rendered the exercise file used in this lesson for you.

3 Open the Lesson_01_final_render.psd file in Adobe Photoshop to examine the final render and compare it to what you saw in the on-canvas Render Preview earlier.

● **Note:** You can switch between Design and Render modes at any time and as often as you wish. Although rendering is usually done at the end of a project, you may occasionally wish to render your work as it progresses so you can get an accurate view of how your project looks at the moment.

4 Click Design to switch back to Design mode, making the 3D content visible again.

Getting help

The Learn icon ⓘ in the far upper-right corner of the screen gives you access to online help content for Dimension, including tutorials, videos, keyboard shortcuts, and galleries of finished work.

Review questions

1   How many files can be open at one time in Dimension?

2   What are the four camera tools for?

3   What is the purpose of Render mode?

4   What is the "floor" that 3D objects rest on called?

Review answers

1   Only one file can be open at a time in Dimension. If you have one file open and then open a second file, the first file will close.

2   The four camera tools (Orbit, Pan, Dolly, and Horizon) all change your view of the scene. They let you examine the scene from different angles, distances, and points of view.

3   Render mode is used to create the final scene with accurate lighting, shadows, reflections, materials, and surface properties. Computers are unable to keep up with accurate rendering in real time as you make edits to a complex scene, so final rendering is a separate process that takes place in Render mode.

4   The imaginary "floor" in a 3D scene is called the Ground Plane.

2 EXPLORING DESIGN MODE

Lesson overview

In this lesson, you'll create a simple 3D scene from scratch and learn the following:

- How to create a new project and specify the canvas size.
- How to change the properties of the background.
- How to import starter assets.
- How to transform 3D objects.
- How to apply materials to objects.
- How to adjust the lighting.
- How to render a scene and produce output that can be used in other programs.

This lesson will take about 45 minutes to complete. To get the lesson files used in this chapter, download them from the web page for this book at www.adobepress.com/DimensionCIB2020. For more information, see "Accessing the lesson files and Web Edition" in the Getting Started section at the beginning of this book.

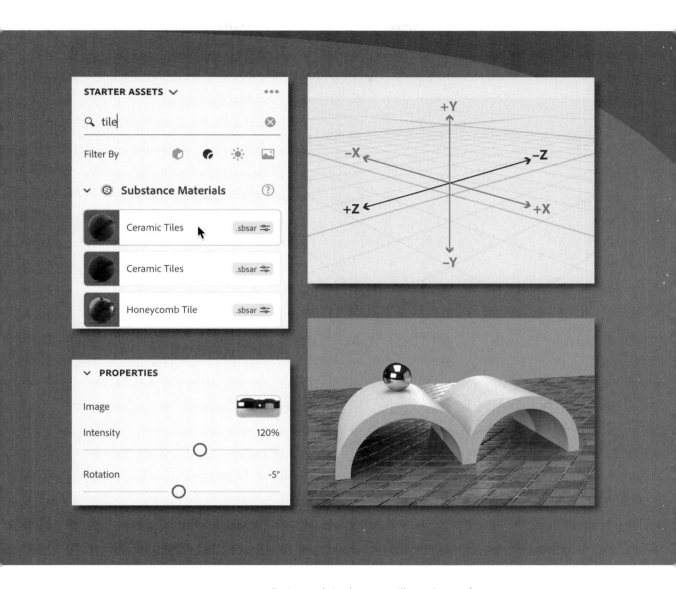

Design mode is where you will spend most of your time in Dimension. This is where you'll position, scale, and rotate models, apply materials to surfaces, and adjust lighting and reflections.

Creating a new project

Starting a new project from scratch in Dimension is as easy as choosing File > New.

1 Choose File > New to create a new document. If you currently have another document open, it will close. If that document isn't saved, you'll be prompted to save it before closing.

Dimension doesn't ask you anything about page size or file size as you create a new file. But you do have control over this.

2 Select the Select tool in the Tools panel (keyboard shortcut: V).

3 Click the 1024 x 768 dimensions that are displayed in the upper-left corner of the canvas. This will select the canvas, and you'll see some options for changing the canvas size appear in the Properties panel on the right.

4 In the Properties panel, change Canvas Size to a width of **3000 px** and a height of **2000 px**.

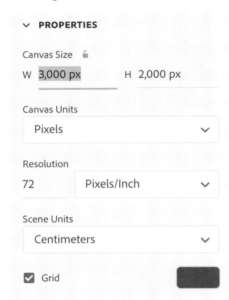

● **Note:** The appropriate values to enter for the canvas width and height depend on the intended use of the final rendered image. If you just need a low-resolution image to use in a small section of a web page, 600 px x 600 px might be sufficient. But an image that will be reproduced on the cover of a print magazine may need to be 4000 px x 4000 px or more. Talk to your web developer or print partner if you need more guidance on this issue. They should be able to tell you the exact pixel dimensions required.

▶ **Tip:** Canvas size significantly influences render time. Use a canvas size that is no larger than necessary.

5 Choose View > Zoom to Fit Canvas to fit the new canvas size on the screen.

Changing the background color

By default, the background of the scene is white. But you can easily change the background color to any value you want.

1 In the Scene panel, select Environment.

2 In the Properties panel, click the property swatch to the right of the word "Background," and enter **135**, **165**, **161** for the RGB values to change the background to a green color.

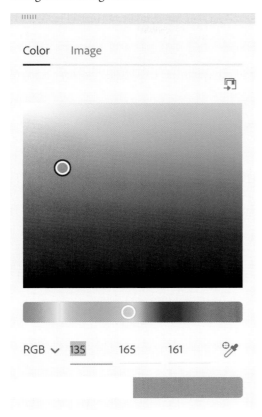

3 Click away from the color picker when you are finished to close it.

4 Choose File > Save, name the file, and save it somewhere you can find it again if necessary.

Working with starter assets

Dimension ships with dozens of "starter assets," including 3D models, materials, lights, and background images you can use to get started creating 3D scenes. You can also use content from Adobe Stock, Creative Cloud Libraries, or your own imported 3D models and 2D images to compose your scenes. In this lesson, we'll work with the starter assets.

Note: Dimension files are automatically assigned the .dn filename extension. Depending on how your operating system is configured, you may or may not see this extension displayed at the end of the filename.

1 Click the Content button  in the lower-left corner of the screen. This button displays and hides the Content panel on the left side of the screen. Click the button until the Content panel is displayed.

The Content panel displays content that you can use in your scene, such as 3D models, materials, lights, and images.

2 If Starter Assets isn't displayed at the top of the Content panel, choose Starter Assets from the menu at the top of the panel.

3 Click the more icon ••• to toggle the panel display between list view and grid view until the models are displayed in list view.

4 Click the model icon ◉ at the top of the panel to display only models in the panel.

5 Type **plane** into the search assets field.

Assets that have "plane" in the name are displayed.

6 Click once on the Plane starter asset to place it into your scene.

● **Note:** When you click a starter asset model, it will always be positioned at the "zero" point in the center of the scene to start. From there, you can move the model to any position in the scene that you wish.

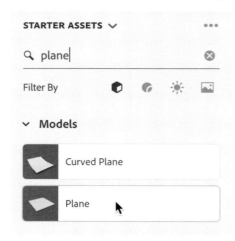

7 Type **pipe** into the search field.

8 Click once on the Half Pipe starter asset to place it into your scene.

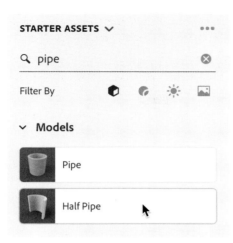

9 Type **sphere** into the search assets field.

10 Click once on the Sphere starter asset to place it into your scene.

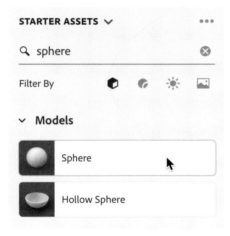

Note that all three models were placed at the same location in the scene, so they are intersecting. You'll fix this in the next steps.

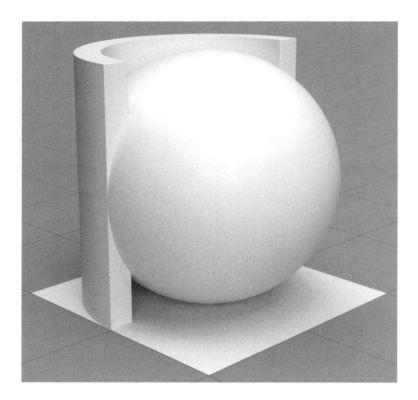

Selecting and transforming objects

The Scene panel makes it easy to determine the various pieces that compose a scene, and it can help you select those pieces. Once a model is selected, it can be moved, scaled, and rotated with the Select tool and the Properties panel. Let's rearrange the models in this scene.

Scaling objects

The Select tool is used not only to select objects, but also to move, rotate, and scale objects in a scene.

1 Double-click the Select tool in the Tools panel.

2 If Align To Scene is on, turn it off. You'll learn more about this option later in this lesson.

3 Select the Plane model in the Scene panel. You'll see the plane model outlined in blue on the canvas to indicate that it is selected.

Understanding the 3D axis

Perhaps you're familiar with the x-axis and y-axis that are used in many 2D design programs. Moving an object along the x-axis moves it from left to right or from right to left. Moving an object along the y-axis moves the object up and down. However, when working in the world of 3D, we need a third axis, the z-axis. Moving an object along the z-axis moves it closer to you or farther away from you.

This is pretty easy to understand and visualize, except that in Dimension the default viewing angle has the x- and z-axes off-center, so you're viewing the objects at an angle. As you move an object closer to you on the z-axis, it also moves right to left across your screen. This can be confusing until you get accustomed to it.

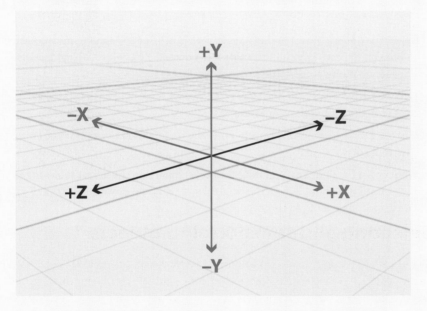

The 3D axes as they are used in the default view of Dimension. The view is off-center, which makes movement along the z-axis easier to see but can be a bit confusing at first.

● **Note:** Exact measurements, and the unit of measure used, aren't terribly important in Dimension, since your primary concern is usually the relative sizes of your models to others in your scene. But measurements can be useful for importing and exporting models to and from other programs at predictable sizes, or for accurately sizing a model based on real-world specifications.

4   Enter values of X=**100 cm**, Y=**0**, and Z=**200 cm** for Size in the Properties panel. This will make the plane model much larger.

Size ⌄ 🔒

X 100 cm   Y 0 cm   Z 200 cm

5   So that you don't accidentally select the Plane model while working with the other models in the scene, hover over Plane in the Scene panel, and click the lock icon 🔒 to the right of the word Plane.

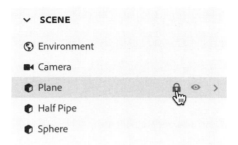

● **Note:** If the Align To Scene option for the Select tool is turned on, you can only scale an object proportionally. If Align To Scene is turned off, hold down the Shift key while scaling to scale proportionally.

6   Select the Sphere model in the Scene panel. You'll see the sphere model outlined in blue on the canvas to indicate that it is selected. The Select tool widget also appears on the selected sphere.

7   Drag the green square on the Select tool widget down a bit. This scales the sphere in the Y direction, flattening it.

8   Choose Edit > Undo Transform to undo the scaling transformation you just applied.

● **Note:** Command+Z (macOS) or Ctrl+Z (Windows) is the keyboard shortcut for undo, exactly like most other Adobe design programs.

9   Hold down the Shift key, and drag the green square on the Select tool widget down until it is about 20% of the original size. Holding down the Shift key constrains the scaling to be proportional.

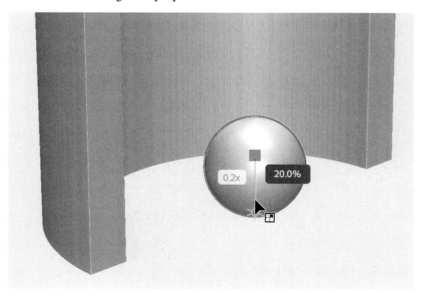

Rotating objects

Just as you used the Select tool to interactively scale an object, you can also use it to rotate objects.

1   Click the Half Pipe model on the canvas to select it.

2   Hold down the Shift key and drag the blue circle on the Select tool widget clockwise until −90° is displayed on the canvas or in the Rotation settings in the Properties panel. Holding down the Shift key constrains the rotation to 15° increments.

● **Note:** If you double-click on the Select tool in the Tools panel, you will discover that there are three additional selection tools to choose from: the Select and Move tool, the Select and Rotate tool, and the Select and Scale tool. Although you can move, scale, and rotate models with the Select tool, these three additional tools provide some extra functionality that is helpful in certain situations. For example, the Select and Move tool allows you to constrain movement to two axes at once.

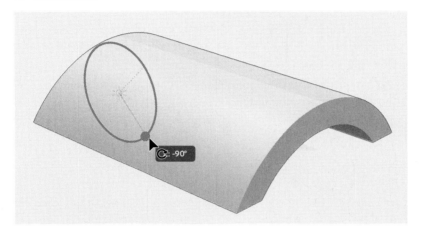

3   Choose Object > Move To Ground so that the bottom of the newly-rotated model sits on the ground plane.

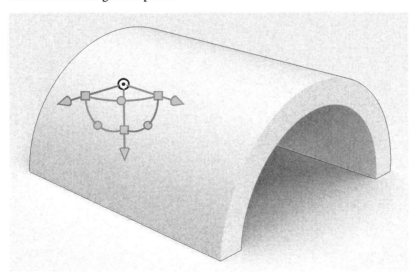

Moving objects

When you rotate a model, the default behavior is that the Select tool widget rotates with the model. Sometimes this is helpful, sometimes not. In this case, the red, green, and blue colors on the widget no longer correspond to the expected colors of the x-, y-, and z-axes. This can make it confusing to move the model in the proper direction.

▶ **Tip:** Press Q any time an object is selected to toggle the Select tool widget between aligning to the scene and aligning to the model.

1   To fix this, double-click the Select tool in the Tools panel.

2   Turn the Align To Scene option on. You'll see the Select tool widget change on the model to align with the x, y, and z directions in the scene.

3   Choose Edit > Duplicate. Note that now there are two half pipe models listed in the Scene panel. Only one is visible on the canvas, as they occupy the same coordinates in the scene.

4   Drag the blue arrow to the right until the two half pipes are positioned side by side and slightly intersecting, as shown below.

▶ **Tip:** Each of the arrows allows you to move an object in only a single direction: x, y, or z. But sometimes you want to freely move an object in both the x and z directions simultaneously. In other words, you want to move an object freely around on the ground plane, without moving it up or down. To do this, drag a model by grabbing the model surface, not one of the arrows. This will constrain movement to only the x and z directions.

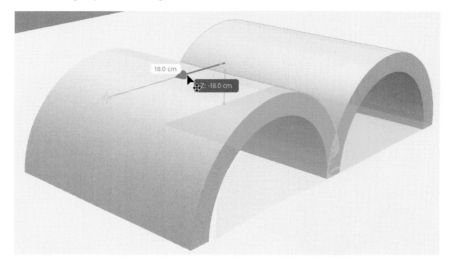

5   Select Camera in the Scene panel.

6   You'll learn more about changing the camera view in another lesson. For now, you'll enter values in the Properties panel so that you can view the models from a different perspective. Enter values of X=**70 cm**, Y=**25 cm**, and Z=**−9 cm** for the Position in the Properties panel.

This may position the canvas so that you only see the plane model. That's OK.

7 Enter values of X=**0°**, Y=**90°**, and Z=**13°** for Rotation in the Properties panel. This will rotate your view so you see the half pipe models straight on.

Rotation

X 0°   Y 90°   Z 13°

8 Select the Sphere model by either clicking on the model on the canvas, or by selecting Sphere in the Scene panel.

9 Drag the green arrow up until the Sphere is positioned somewhere above the half pipe models.

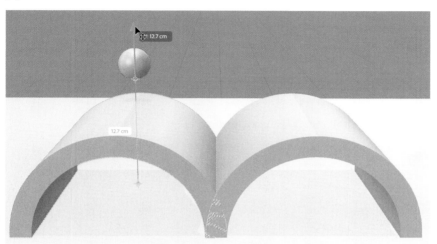

10 Drag the "Pivot Handle" (the black and white circle located on the Select tool widget at the bottom of the sphere model) down to the surface of the half pipe model. You'll see that when you drag the pivot handle around the surface of the half pipe, the sphere follows the contours on the surface of the model. This feature is really helpful for accurately positioning one model on the surface of another.

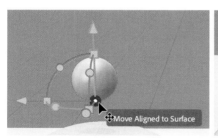
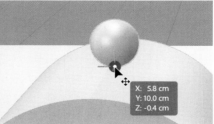

11 To select all three models at once, drag a selection boundary that touches the sphere and both half pipe models.

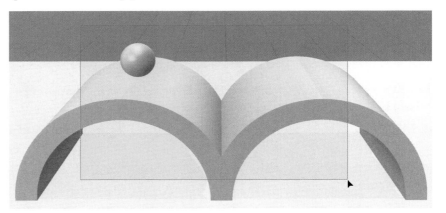

12 Choose Camera > Frame Selection to fill the screen with the three models.

13 Choose Edit > Deselect All

14 Select the Orbit tool (keyboard shortcut: 1).

15 Drag down and slightly to the right until the camera angle is slightly offset.

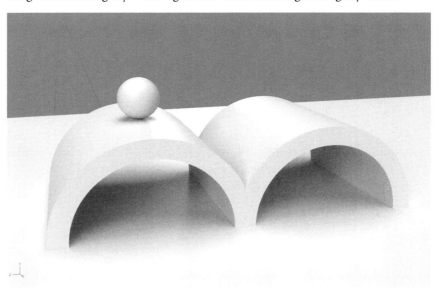

Applying materials to models

When you import a 3D model into a scene, it will arrive with whatever materials were applied to the model when it was created. But Dimension allows you to adjust the properties of materials or to apply entirely new materials to a model. This lesson is a brief introduction to materials. You'll dive more deeply into materials in a later lesson.

1 Select one of the Half Pipe models with the Select tool.

2 Hold down the Shift key, and select the other Half Pipe model. Holding down the Shift key allows you to select more than one model at a time.

3 In the Content panel on the left side of the screen, click the X icon ⊗ next to the search field to clear the previous search term.

4 Click the Materials icon 🝆 to view only materials in the panel.

5 Click the More icon ••• in the upper-right corner of the panel, and choose Toggle List/Grid View until the materials are displayed in list view.

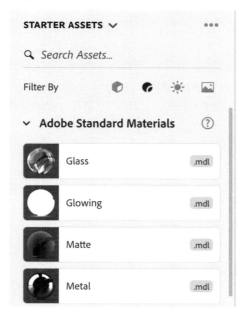

6 Experiment by selecting different materials in the list to apply them to the Half Pipe models.

7 Type **concrete** into the search field, and select the Cracked Concrete material to apply it to the surface of the Half Pipe models.

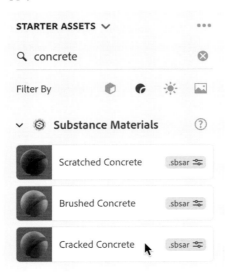

8 Select the Sphere model.

9 Type **metal** into the search field, and select the Metal material to apply it to the surface of the Sphere model.

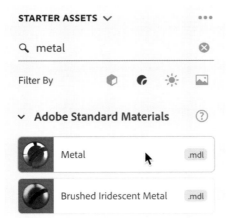

10 Choose Edit > Deselect All.

11 In the Scene panel, click the lock icon 🔒 next to Plane to unlock the Plane model.

12 Select the Plane model in the Scene panel.

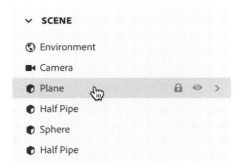

13 Type **tile** into the search field, and select the green Ceramic Tiles material to apply it to the surface of the Plane model.

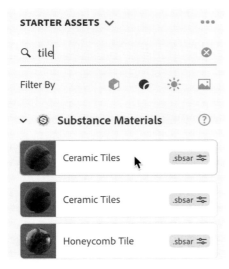

14 In the Properties panel, enter **30°** for the Offset Rotation.

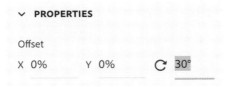

15 In the Properties panel, change the Tiles Amount to 50.

16 Choose Edit > Deselect All to deselect the Plane model.

17 Click the Render Preview icon  to see a more accurate view of your scene. You can leave Render Preview on for the rest of this lesson.

Adjusting the lighting

Dimension scenes can contain two different types of lighting: the environment light and directional lights. Environment light is the ambient light that surrounds the scene. Directional lights can be added to, or used in place of, environment light to create strong directional shadows and reflections. Both of these lights can be customized in many ways.

Adjusting the environment light

In this lesson you will fine-tune the location and color of the environment light.

1 Select Environment in the Scene panel.

2 Under Environment, select Environment Light.

3 In the Properties panel, enter **120%** for Intensity, and **−5°** for Rotation. This will make the light brighter, and move it a bit to the right.

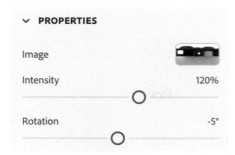

4   In the Properties panel, under Environment Light, select the Colorize option.

5   By default, the Colorize option is set to white. Click the color swatch next to
    Colorize and choose a color with RGB values of **255, 255, 232**. This will apply a
    slight yellow warmth to the environment light. When you are finished, click away
    from the color picker to dismiss it.

Adding sunlight

In this lesson you'll add a single directional light to the scene that simulates sunlight. You'll learn a lot more about lighting in another lesson.

1 In the Content panel on the left side of the screen, click the X icon ⊗ next to the search field to clear the previous search term.

2 Click the Lights icon ☀ to view only lights in the panel.

3 Select Sun to add a light that simulates sunlight to the scene.

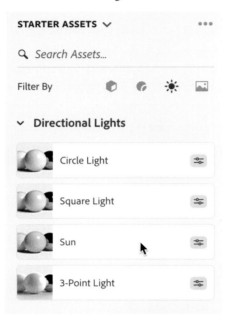

4 In the Properties panel, enter **−33** for the Rotation value, **14°** for Height, and **30%** for Cloudiness.

5 Choose File > Save.

Introduction to scene rendering

The file you've been working on is saved as a Dimension file. The Dimension file format can't be opened with Photoshop, placed in InDesign or Illustrator, or printed to a color printer. Getting output in a useful form requires that you render the scene. You'll render this scene in this lesson, and learn much more about rendering in a later lesson.

1 Click the Render tab at the upper-left corner of the screen.

2 In the Properties panel under Render Settings, select Local.

3 Make a note of the filename.

4 Choose Low (Fast) for the Quality.

5 Choose PSD (16 Bits/Channel) for the export format.

6 For Save To, choose an export location.

7 Click the Render button.

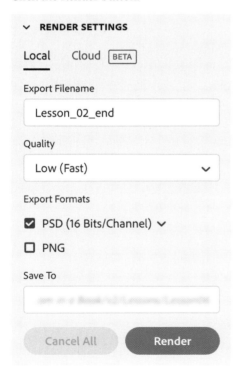

8   Wait for the render to complete. The time needed depends on the speed of your computer. Rendering can be a slow process. Be patient.

    You can't do anything else in Dimension while the render is taking place, but you can use other programs on your computer while the render is finishing.

9   When the render is complete, open and view the completed PSD file in Photoshop.

10 In Photoshop, choose Image > Image Size, and you'll see that the rendered PSD file is 3000 px x 2000 px, as you specified for the canvas size when you began the project.

11 Zoom in on the image in Photoshop. You'll see that the image contains a lot of "noise," particularly noticeable in the cast shadows. This is because we chose a low quality and fast speed for the render settings. A high-quality, slow-speed render would give much nicer results but take considerably longer.

Review questions

1 What filename extension is added to Dimension files?

2 When, and where, do you specify the canvas size in Dimension?

3 When you add a starter asset to a scene, where is the asset positioned in the scene?

4 Moving an object along the z-axis moves the object in what direction?

5 What are two ways to rotate a 3D model?

6 What are the two types of lights built into Dimension?

Review answers

1 The filename extension for Dimension files is .dn.

2 The canvas size can be specified in the Properties panel after a file is created.

3 When you add a starter asset to a scene, it is added to the "middle" of the scene, at X=0, Y=0, and Z=0.

4 In Dimension's default camera view, moving an object on the z-axis moves it closer to, or farther away from, the camera.

5 Select the model with the Select tool and then either enter values in the Properties panel or drag one of the circles on the Select tool widget displayed on the model.

6 Environment light and directional lights.

3 CHANGING YOUR VIEW OF THE SCENE: WORKING WITH THE CAMERA

Lesson overview

In this lesson, you'll manipulate your view of an existing 3D scene and learn the following:

- How the Orbit, Pan, Dolly, and Horizon tools work.

- When and why to use the camera tools.

- How to use bookmarks to save camera angles.

- How to simulate camera depth of field in a scene.

This lesson will take about 45 minutes to complete. To get the lesson files used in this chapter, download them from the web page for this book at www.adobepress.com/DimensionCIB2020. For more information, see "Accessing the lesson files and Web Edition" in the Getting Started section at the beginning of this book.

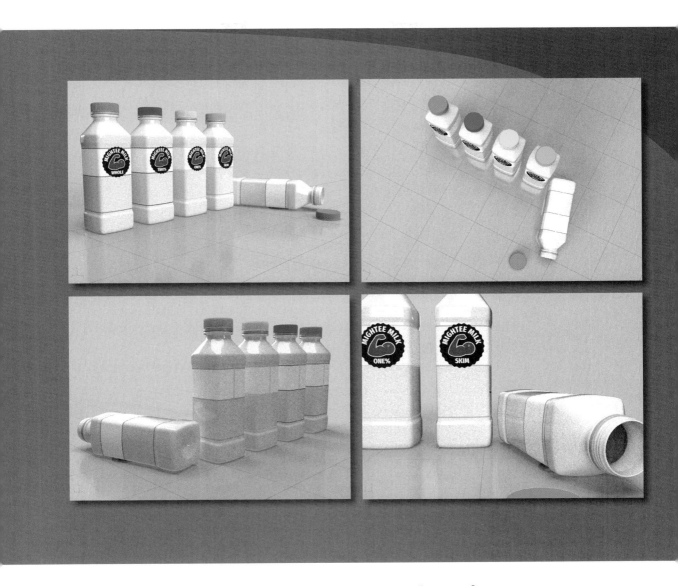

The Camera tools in Dimension allow you to fly around a scene and view it from different angles and perspectives.

What is the camera?

While you're composing a 3D scene, you'll often need to examine the scene from a variety of angles. For example, if you are trying to position a vase precisely on a tabletop, you may need to view the table with your eye level even with the top of the table so you can see when the vase is resting on the tabletop. When looking down on the table from above, it is difficult to determine whether the vase is "floating" above the table or resting upon it.

Dimension uses the concept of a virtual "camera" through which you view the scene. There are four camera-related tools:

- The Orbit tool
- The Pan tool
- The Dolly tool
- The Horizon tool

In this lesson, we'll look closely at how these tools work.

Saving a camera bookmark

Camera bookmarks provide a way to save a specific view of your scene so that you can quickly and easily return to the view later after you've changed your view with the camera tools. In this exercise, you'll open a file and save a camera bookmark of your initial view of the scene.

1. Launch Adobe Dimension.

2. Click Open, or choose File > Open.

3. Select the file named Lesson_03_begin.dn, which is in the Lessons > Lesson03 folder that you copied onto your hard disk, and then click Open.

4. Click the Camera Bookmarks icon 📷 at the top of the screen.

5. Click the plus icon ➕ to create a new bookmark.

6. To rename the bookmark, type **Starting view** and press Return/Enter.

Using the Orbit tool

The Orbit tool does what its name suggests: it lets you "orbit" around the scene, examining it from different angles. You can move up, down, clockwise, and counter-clockwise around your scene. And, unlike in real life, you can even move the camera "underground" and view the scene looking up from beneath the ground plane. In other words, imagine that the ground plane is ice on a lake. With the Orbit tool, you can dive into the lake, point the camera up at the scene that is sitting on the frozen surface of the ice, and view the scene through the transparent ice.

1   Select the Orbit tool in the Tools panel (keyboard shortcut: 1).

2   Drag from right to left across the screen to "fly" around the scene in a counterclockwise direction.

3   Choose Camera > Camera Undo to reset to the initial view.

4   Drag from left to right across the screen to orbit in a clockwise direction.

5   Drag from the bottom of the screen to the top of the screen to view the scene from below the ground plane.

▶ **Tip:** If you have a two-button mouse, you can also drag with the right mouse button while any tool is selected to use the Orbit tool.

As we saw in a previous lesson, the grid lines on the ground plane are black on top and red underneath. This is your visual cue as to where you "are." If you see red lines, you're looking up through the ground plane (the floor). If you see black lines, you're looking down on the ground plane.

6   Click the Camera Bookmarks icon.

7   Click "Starting view" to return to the initial view of the scene.

Examining the scene with the Orbit tool

Changing your view of the scene with the Orbit tool is often helpful when you are attempting to precisely align objects.

1   Drag with the Orbit tool until you are viewing the models straight on from the front, similar to this:

2   Choose Camera > Frame All. This command automatically manipulates the camera so that all the models in the scene are centered on the screen and fill the screen.

3   Click the Camera Bookmarks icon 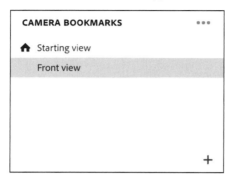.

4   Click the plus icon ➕ to create a new bookmark.

5   To rename the bookmark, type **Front view** and press Return/Enter.

From this angle, you can see that the space between the red and blue bottles is larger than the space between the rest of the bottles. Let's fix this.

6   Select the Select tool (keyboard shortcut: V).

7   Click the "Whole milk – red" model in the Scene panel to select the bottle with the red cap. Selecting the model in the Scene panel ensures that you get the entire bottle selected, not just the body or the bottle cap.

8   Drag the blue arrowhead to the right until the bottles are equally spaced.

9 Select the Orbit tool (keyboard shortcut: 1).

10 Drag with the Orbit tool until you're viewing the models from the left end, similar to this:

Tip: After you begin dragging with the Orbit tool, you can add the Shift key to constrain your motion to a vertical or horizontal orbit.

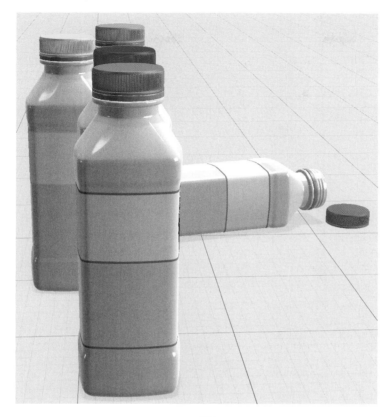

11 Click the Camera Bookmarks icon 📷.

12 Click the plus icon ➕ to create a new bookmark.

13 To rename the bookmark, type **Left end view** and press Return/Enter.

From this angle, you can see that one of the upright bottles isn't lined up with the rest of the bottles. Let's fix this.

14 Select the Select tool (keyboard shortcut: V).

15 Click the "1 percent – yellow" model in the Scene panel to select it.

16 Drag the red arrowhead to the right until the bottles are lined up.

17 Click the Camera Bookmarks icon [icon].

18 Click "Starting view" to return to the initial view of the scene.

Using the Pan tool

The Pan tool is used to move the camera left, right, up, or down. Panning is different from orbiting. When you pan the camera from right to left, it is as if you are simply walking by the scene in a straight line, not curving around the scene. When you pan from the top of the screen to the bottom of the screen, the horizon stays fixed in place, and it appears as if you are climbing a ladder.

1 Select the Pan tool (keyboard shortcut: 2).

2 Drag from right to left across the screen to pan the scene from right to left.

3 Click the Camera Undo icon [icon] (located to the left of the Camera Bookmarks icon) to reset to the initial view.

4   Drag from the bottom of the screen to the top of the screen to view the scene from below the ground plane. Note that the imaginary horizon remains fixed on the screen when you pan vertically.

5   Click the Camera Bookmarks icon 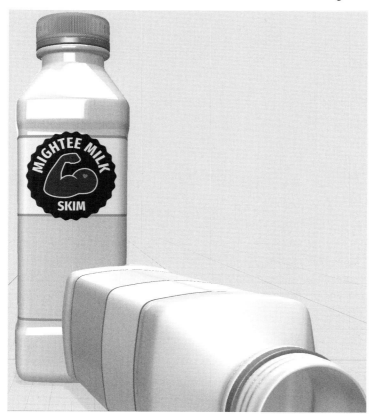.

6   Click "Front view" to go to the front view of the scene.

7   Select the Select tool (keyboard shortcut: V).

8   Click the "Whole milk – red" model in the Scene panel to select it.

9   Choose Camera > Frame Selection.

10 This will reposition the camera to center the single bottle on the screen.

11 Select the Pan tool (keyboard shortcut: 2).

12 Drag from right to left across the screen to pan the scene from right to left until the green and purple bottles are visible on the screen.

From this view, you can see that the two bottles are intersecting. Let's fix this.

Tip: If you have a three-button mouse, you can drag with the middle mouse button to pan the camera. (On some mice, the scroll wheel acts as a third button when pressed.)

13 Select the Select tool (keyboard shortcut: V).

14 Select the "Half – purple" model in the Scene panel.

15 Drag the blue arrow to the right until the bottles no longer intersect.

Using the Dolly tool

● **Note:** Depending on how your mouse preferences are configured on your computer, the direction you drag the Dolly tool may be inverted from what is described here.

▶ **Tip:** You can also use the scroll wheel to engage the Dolly tool when any other tool is selected.

The Dolly tool moves the camera toward the scene or away from the scene. The name of this tool comes from the wheeled camera "dollies" used in film and television production.

1 Select the Dolly tool (keyboard shortcut: 3).

2 Drag from the bottom to the top of the screen to move the camera toward the scene, enlarging your view of the models.

3 Drag from the top of the screen to the bottom to move the camera away from the scene, which makes the models appear smaller.

4 Click the Camera Bookmarks icon.

5 Click "Starting view" to return to the initial view of the scene.

Using the Horizon tool

The Horizon tool allows you to move the horizon in your scene up or down or to adjust the tilt of the horizon. This tool is particularly useful when you are trying to position a 3D model in a 2D image.

1   Choose File > Import > Image As Background.

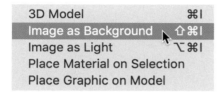

2   Select the Simple_background.psd file in the Lessons > Lesson03 folder that you copied onto your hard disk and then click Open.

3   In the Actions panel, click Match Image.

4   Select the "Resize Canvas To" option, and deselect the "Create Lights" option.

In this case, note that the Match Camera Perspective option isn't available. This is because this background image doesn't contain any perspective lines to help Dimension determine a vanishing point.

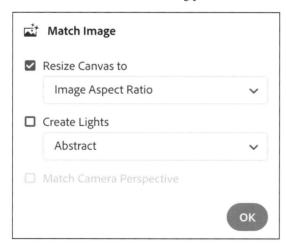

5   Click OK.

6 Select the Horizon tool (keyboard shortcut: N).

Because this background image doesn't contain any perspective lines to help Dimension determine a vanishing point and horizon, you'll have to set the horizon manually.

7 Drag the middle handle on the blue horizon line on the image until it is lined up with the "horizon" between the tan and gray areas of the background image. Note that the bottles move as you move the horizon line.

8 Grab the round selection handle on the right end of the horizon line and drag up. This is what you would need to do if the horizon in your scene were tilted.

9   Click the Camera Undo icon 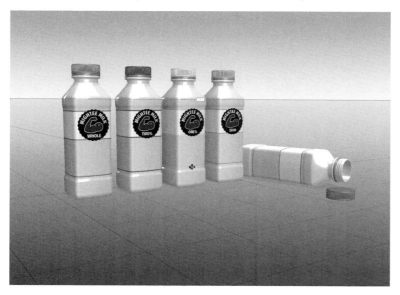 to return the view to a horizontal horizon.

Now the bottles are positioned too low in the scene. You can fix this with the Horizon tool.

10 With your mouse positioned somewhere on the bottles, drag up to lower the camera until the tops of the bottles are above the horizon. Note that the horizon line remains in place as you do this.

11 If necessary, select the Dolly tool again, and drag up on the image to enlarge the bottles further. Then switch to the Horizon tool and drag the bottles so that the scene looks something like this:

12 Click the Camera Bookmarks icon 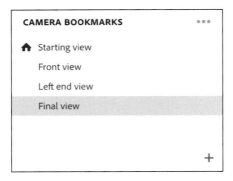.

13 Click the plus icon $\boxed{+}$ to create a new bookmark.

14 To rename the bookmark, type **Final view** and press Return/Enter.

CAMERA BOOKMARKS   • • •

🏠 Starting view

Front view

Left end view

Final view

+

15 Select the Orbit tool (keyboard shortcut: 1).

16 Drag to the right and up a bit to rotate your angle of view.

17 Select the Horizon tool (keyboard shortcut: N). Your horizon line is probably now out of position and no longer lined up with the horizon in the background image. This is because the Orbit tool adjusts only your view of the 3D models in the scene, not the background image.

18 Use the Horizon tool to reposition the horizon line on the background image. You may also need to drag down on the bottles with the Horizon tool to raise the camera for a better view after you've moved the horizon line.

Using camera bookmarks

As you've seen, camera bookmarks are a handy way to save camera angles so that you can quickly return to the same angle at any time. There are a few more details about camera bookmarks that you should know.

1 Earlier, you saved a camera bookmark named "Final view." But you made a few changes to the camera angle and perspective after saving the bookmark. To update the bookmark, click the Camera Bookmarks icon .

2 Hover over the "Final view" bookmark and then click the Update To Current View icon 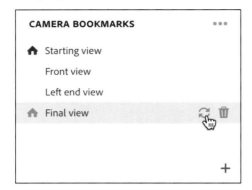 to update the bookmark to match the current camera angle and perspective.

● **Note:** There is no limit to the number of camera bookmarks that you can save in a Dimension file.

▶ **Tip:** Use the Page Up and Page Down keys to cycle through each view in the Camera Bookmarks panel.

▶ **Tip:** Another reason to save a camera bookmark is that when you render your scene, you can tell Dimension to render a specific camera view. So, you could save several different camera views of a scene and then render all the views at once.

3 The bookmark named "Starting view" has a Home icon ⌂ next to it. This means that this is the view that the Camera > Switch To Home View command (keyboard shortcut: Command+B/Ctrl+B) will switch to. Hover over the space to the left of the "Final view" bookmark and click the light gray home icon to make this view the Home view.

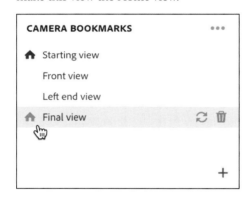

Simulating depth of field

Depth of field is a photographic term that refers to how much of the scene being photographed will be in focus when the shutter is clicked. Depending on the lens and the lighting, the depth of field may be virtually infinite (so that everything is in focus), or it may be shallow (so that only objects at a specific distance from the lens are in focus and everything else is blurry). You can simulate this photographic principle with the Focus controls in Dimension.

1   Click the Render Preview icon 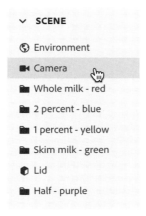 to display a more accurate view of your scene.

2   In the Scene panel, select Camera.

3   In the Properties panel, toggle the Focus option on by clicking the switch to the right of the word "Focus." This will open the Focus controls.

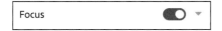

4   Click the Set Focus Point button and then click the label on the yellow bottle. You'll see an icon that indicates the focus point placed on the scene.

5   Enter a value of **10** for Blur Amount.

● **Note:** If you need to reposition the focus point, you'll need to click the Set Focus Point button again and click a new location for the focus point. In other words, the focus point indicator on the Canvas cannot be dragged and moved.

6 A rough preview of the result displays on the canvas. Here is what the final render of the scene looks like.

Review questions

1 Which tool moves the camera closer to, or farther away from, the scene?

2 What does the Pan tool do?

3 What is the purpose of saving a camera bookmark?

4 Is there a limit to the number of camera bookmarks you can save?

5 What are the Dimension options called that let you simulate camera depth of field?

Review answers

1 The Dolly tool allows you to move the camera closer to or farther from the scene.

2 The Pan tool is used to move the camera left, right, up, or down. As you do this, the horizon stays in place.

3 You save a camera bookmark so that you can quickly return to a particular view of a scene at any time. Camera bookmarks are also useful for saving specific views to be rendered later.

4 No, there is no limit to the number of camera bookmarks that can be saved with a file.

5 The Focus options in the Properties panel will simulate camera depth of field in your scene.

4 EXPLORING RENDER MODE

Lesson overview

In this lesson, you'll explore how to render a 3D scene and learn the following:

- The three different places where rendering takes place in Dimension, and how they differ from one another.

- The trade-offs between render speed and quality.

- How to get a quick "good enough" render when you are in a hurry.

- How to achieve the highest-quality rendered image.

 This lesson will take about 45 minutes to complete. To get the lesson files used in this chapter, download them from the web page for this book at www.adobepress.com/DimensionCIB2020. For more information, see "Accessing the lesson files and Web Edition" in the Getting Started section at the beginning of this book.

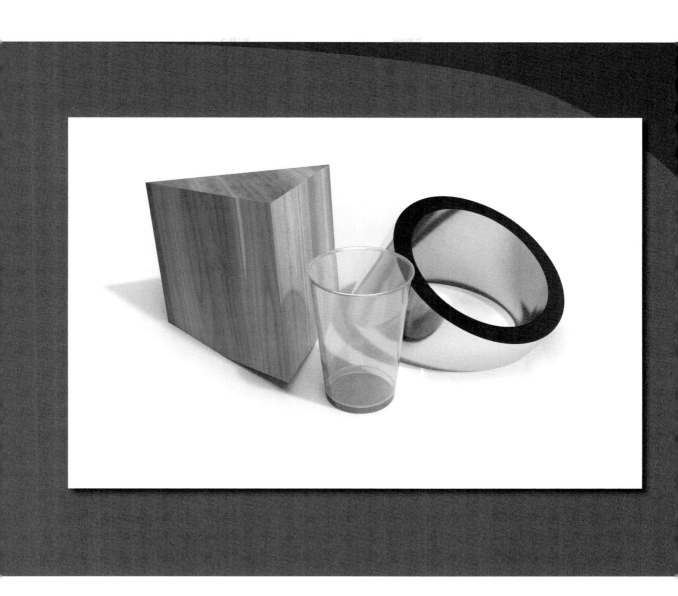

Dimension's Render mode produces a 2D scene from 3D models, complete with realistic light, shadow, materials, and reflections.

What is rendering?

Rendering refers to the process of producing a realistic-looking 2D scene from a 3D model or models.

Dimension uses a form of rendering called *ray tracing*. A high-level explanation of ray tracing is that the computer calculates a path from each pixel in the scene back to the camera and calculates the color of that pixel based on the environment lighting, the directional lights, the material applied to the surface, and reflections from other objects. This requires a lot of computing horsepower, and is far too complex for today's computers to accurately perform in real time as a scene is edited.

Because of this, Dimension offers three levels of rendering: a real-time rough rendering that Dimension performs as you edit a 3D scene, a blended render preview that automatically switches between a high-quality ray-traced render and real-time rendering as you edit, and the final Render mode.

Exploring real-time rendering

As you position 3D models in Design mode, Dimension displays a basic preview of the resulting scene on the canvas. Because an accurate rendering of the scene is so time-consuming, this real-time preview is only a rough approximation of what the final scene will look like. Effects that will appear especially rough in the real-time preview include:

- Shadows cast by 3D models on the ground plane.
- Glass and other semi-transparent materials applied to 3D model surfaces.
- The camera depth of field.

Things that don't display at all in the on-canvas preview include:

- Reflections cast by one model onto another model.
- Reflections cast by models on the ground plane.

In this lesson you'll explore a finished scene and observe some of these limitations in the real-time rendering of the scene.

1 Launch Adobe Dimension.

2 Click Open, or choose File > Open.

3 Select the file named Lesson_04_begin.dn, which is in the Lessons > Lesson04 folder that you copied onto your hard disk, and then click Open.

4 If the Render Preview icon ▦ in the upper-right corner of the work area is selected, click the icon to turn Render Preview off.

5　Note some of the limitations of the real-time rendering of this scene. The shadows being cast by the 3D models are hard-edged.

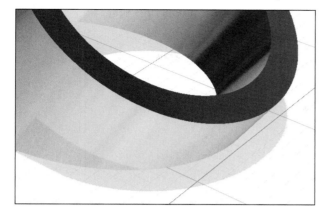

You'd expect to see some part of the wood Prism model reflected in the shiny silver surface of the Pipe model, but no reflection is visible.

6　Select Environment in the Scene panel.

7   If the Ground Plane options are hidden in the Properties panel, click the disclosure icon $\boxed{>}$ to the left of Ground Plane to reveal the options.

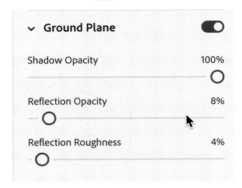

Because there is a Reflection Opacity value of 8%, you'd expect to see a slight reflection of the 3D models in the ground plane, but no reflection appears in the real-time preview.

The bottom line is that the real-time preview is useful primarily as a way to judge the position, size, and placement of 3D models within a scene. To see materials, surfaces, and lighting accurately, you must use the blended render preview.

Exploring blended render preview

The blended render preview automatically switches in and out of an accurate ray-traced render and the faster, less accurate real-time preview on an as-needed basis as you make edits to your scene.

1   Click the Render Preview icon ⊞ in the upper-right corner of the work area.

2   Wait for the render preview to update. Note the rough, speckled "noise" in the shadows in the render preview. This will diminish and the preview will become more accurate as Dimension continues to render the scene.

3   Select the cup with the Select tool, and use the blue arrow on the Select tool widget to move the cup model to the right a bit. As you do this, you'll see the ray-traced preview turn off and the real-time preview turn on. As soon as you let go of the cup, the ray-traced preview will begin again.

Note that the render preview shows the wood Prism object reflected in the shiny surface of the Pipe model.

4 In the Content panel, click the Lights icon ☀ to view only lights in the panel.

5 Select Sun to add a light that simulates sunlight to the scene.

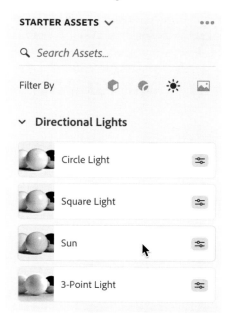

6 In the Properties panel, enter **145%** for the sunlight Intensity, **100°** for the Rotation, **55°** for the Height, and **35%** for the Cloudiness. As you adjust the

values, you'll see Dimension switch back to the real-time preview, and return to the ray-traced preview when you're finished.

Depending on the speed of your computer and the complexity and size of your scene, you'll need to decide when to switch the blended render mode on and off to suit your needs.

You can tweak the performance of the blended render mode by right-clicking on the Render Preview icon ▓ . This allows you to choose full, half, or quarter resolution for the render preview, and to turn off noise reduction. Reducing the resolution and/or turning off noise reduction can greatly speed up the ray-traced rendering, but of course the preview will not be as accurate.

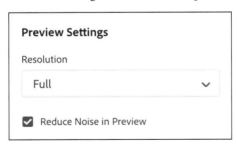

Using render preview snapshots

You can take a snapshot of the ray-traced render preview at any time. Depending on your needs, if Dimension has been working on the render preview for awhile, the render might be good enough for your output requirements.

1   Click the Share icon 📤 in the upper-right corner of the screen.

2 Click the disk icon 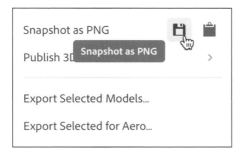. (Or, you could click the clipboard icon to copy the image to the macOS or Windows clipboard.)

3 Choose a filename and a location, and click the Save button.

Exploring Render mode

To really see an accurate view of the scene, the scene must be rendered in Render mode.

1 Before you go to Render mode, click the Camera Bookmarks icon at the top of the screen.

You'll see that there are five bookmarks saved with this file.

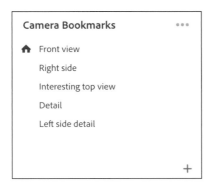

2 Click each bookmark in turn to see what each view looks like.

3 When you're finished, click the "Front view" bookmark to return to that view.

4 To enter Render mode, click the Render tab at the top of the screen.

5 Select Local at the top of the Render Settings panel.

6 You'll see all five of the camera bookmarks displayed at the top of the panel. This handy feature lets you render multiple camera views of a scene all at once. Since rendering can be very time consuming, this provides a way to queue up multiple renders of a scene and let them run overnight or while you're at lunch.

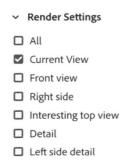

For now, just leave "Current View" selected.

7 Type **My_Lesson_04_end LOW** in the Export Filename field. Dimension appends the name of the view to the end of the filename, so this file will be exported as My_Lesson_04_end LOW-Current View.

8 In the Quality setting, choose Low (Fast).

9 Deselect PSD under Export Format, and select PNG.

10 If you want to change the export location, click the blue export path and choose
   a new export location.

11 Click Render.

12 Wait for the render to finish.

   The render took about four minutes on my MacBook Pro. If you don't want to wait
   for the render to finish, I've saved a copy of the rendered file for you in the lesson
   files (Lesson_04_end LOW-Current View.png).

13 Now change the Quality setting to High (Slow).

14 Change the filename to **My_Lesson_04_end HIGH**.

15 Click Render.

   ∨ **Render Settings**

   Export Filename

   | My_ Lesson_04_end HIGH |

   Quality

   | High (Slow)   ∨ |

   Wait for the render to finish. This render took about 25 minutes on my
   computer. If you don't want to wait for it to finish, I've saved a copy of the file for
   you in the lesson files (Lesson_04_end HIGH-Current View.png).

● **Note:** Although you can't continue to work in Dimension while a file is being rendered, you can continue to work in other applications on your computer. If you have notifications turned on in your operating system, you'll receive a notification when the render is complete.

▶ **Tip:** While a file is rendering, you can click the Snapshot icon 🔲 at any time to save a PNG or PSD file of the render in progress. Since the render engine performs multiple "passes" through the scene, a partially completed render may be far enough along to give you a good idea of what the final render will look like.

While a file is rendering, the Render Status panel displays a progress bar that provides a rough approximation of how much of the render has completed.

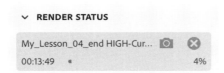

Understanding render speed and quality

As you've seen, there are three Quality settings available in Render mode: Low (Fast), Medium, and High (Slow). How do these settings compare?

1   Use Adobe Photoshop to open the two files you just rendered or, if you wish, the Lesson_04_end HIGH-Current View.png and Lesson_04_end LOW-Current view.png files included in the lesson files.

2   Examine the files closely. You'll see that the low-quality render (on the left in the accompanying image) contains a lot of noise, which is particularly visible in the shadows. The high-quality render (on the right) contains much smoother shadows and less noise.

You'll need to determine which render quality you need to suit your needs. Rendering can be very slow. This is a relatively simple file. Larger, more complex files can take much, much longer to render.

Factors that influence render speed

The time it takes for Dimension to render a scene can vary significantly from file to file and is influenced by a number of factors. I've ranked these factors from most significant (hardware) to least significant (memory).

Hardware

The speed of the CPU (central processing unit) on your computer has a big effect on render speed. Generally speaking, the faster your processor, the faster the rendering. Modern CPUs with more cores and higher speeds will render fastest.

Materials

More than any other factor, the combination of materials used in a scene has a huge impact on the length of time it takes to render the scene. In general, translucent materials like glass, liquids, or gels render more slowly than other materials.

Reflections

Reflections on shiny surfaces slow rendering. Reflections include objects that are reflected on the shiny surfaces of other objects around them, as well as a ground plane with a Reflection Opacity greater than zero so that models reflect on it.

Focus

The Focus feature, which simulates depth of field—causing some objects to be blurred and others to be crisp—slows rendering times.

Canvas size

The total pixel dimensions of the canvas affect render speed. The more pixels, the slower the render time.

Number and complexity of models

Surprisingly, the complexity and number of models in the scene don't have a very large effect on render speeds.

Memory

The amount of memory you have installed on your computer has little effect on rendering speeds.

Using render export formats

So far, you've been rendering into the PNG format. But you may have noted that you can also choose PSD as an output format. What are the advantages to rendering as a PSD file?

There is no difference in the quality of the rendered image between the two formats. The difference is that the PSD file will contain extra layers and masks that make it easier to edit the scene in Photoshop later if necessary. You'll learn about this in more detail in a later lesson. But for now, open the lesson file named Lesson_04_end HIGH-Current View.psd and examine the Layers panel in Photoshop to view the extra data included in a PSD render.

Understanding cloud rendering (beta)

Choosing Cloud under Render Settings in the Properties panel lets you off-load rendering duties to Adobe's servers, freeing your computer from this processor-intensive task. This option offers all the same options and controls as a local render. This is currently a Beta feature.

- Cloud renders are saved to your Creative Cloud Files storage.

- Cloud Render is free, and works on a credit system. Creative Cloud members receive a certain number of credits per month, which can be redeemed for cloud renders.

- Cloud renders are limited to a maximum scene dimension of 4000 x 4000 pixels. If your scene dimensions exceed this, you receive a warning before the image is uploaded to the cloud renderer, and the image is downsampled to fit within 4000 x 4000 pixels.

Review questions

1   What is ray tracing?

2   What are the three places in Dimension where a 3D scene is rendered into 2D?

3   Do reflections appear in the real-time preview?

4   What is the most visible limitation of the ray-traced render preview?

Review answers

1   Ray tracing refers to the rendering method used by the rendering engine built into Dimension. Ray tracing performs complex mathematical calculations to determine the precise color of each pixel in the scene.

2   Dimension performs rendering in three places: the real-time preview, the ray-traced render preview, and Render mode.

3   No. Reflections cast by objects on the ground plane, and cast by objects on other objects, will not appear in the real-time preview.

4   Because it renders as quickly as possible, the render preview displays a lot of noise, especially in shadows.

5 FINDING AND USING 3D MODELS

Lesson overview

In this lesson, you'll import models from various sources and learn the following:

- Why the starter assets included with Dimension are a good place to begin when learning Dimension.

- How to use Adobe Stock to find 3D objects.

- How to download a model from Adobe Stock and use it in a scene.

- How to import 3D models in other industry-standard file formats into Dimension.

- How to assemble models into a realistic scene.

This lesson will take about 45 minutes to complete. To get the lesson files used in this chapter, download them from the web page for this book at www.adobepress.com/DimensionCIB2020. For more information, see "Accessing the lesson files and Web Edition" in the Getting Started section at the beginning of this book.

3D models from a variety of sources, including Adobe
Stock, can be downloaded and then imported into
your scene.

Using starter assets

As you saw in an earlier lesson, Dimension includes dozens of 3D models, materials, lights, and background images you can use to get started creating 3D scenes. The 3D models included with Dimension as starter assets are excellent for getting started with 3D scene building. They are carefully optimized for use with Dimension—they will import into a scene at a reliable size, arrive at consistent coordinates in the scene, and feature clearly named surfaces and materials.

Once you begin looking elsewhere for 3D models, you'll soon discover that model quality varies widely. You'll find that some models consist of a low number of polygons, so curved surfaces appear as a sequence of straight lines. You might find that a model of a bottle is made up of only a single unit, with the bottle cap not created as a separate object. A model creator can do any number of things that make it difficult to work with a model in Dimension or any other program.

Even well-designed, high-quality models are sometimes saved in such a way that, when placed in Dimension, they appear upside down, rotated, huge, or tiny, or behave in some other unpredictable fashion.

For these reasons, until you become comfortable working in Dimension, it's easiest to work with the starter assets.

Examining a starter asset

Some of the starter assets are simple objects that consist of just a single model. But other assets are carefully constructed of multiple models grouped together and clearly labeled to make it easy to work with them. Let's examine one such starter asset and see how it is assembled.

1   Choose File > New to create a new document. If you currently have another document open, it will close. If that document isn't saved, you'll be prompted to save it before closing.

2   Click the Add And Import Content icon ⊕ at the top of the Tools panel, and choose Starter Assets. This displays the Content panel on the left side of the screen and displays the starter content in the panel.

3   If any of the "Filter By" icons are selected, click once on each selected icon to deselect it.

4   Type **laptop** into the Search field at the top of the Content panel.

5   Click the 16:10 Laptop model to place the model in the scene. Note that the laptop neatly lands in the center of the scene.

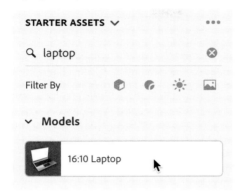

6   Choose Camera > Frame Selection so that you can see the entire laptop model on the screen.

7   In the Scene panel, note that the laptop model is a group of eight models, each clearly labeled.

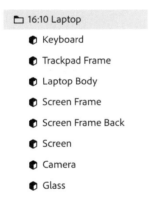

▶ **Tip:** The keyboard shortcut for Camera > Frame Selection is F. As a bonus, if nothing is selected, the F shortcut acts just like Camera > Frame All, changing the camera view so that you can see all the models in the scene.

In the Scene panel, the white folder icon [⬜] indicates a group that is open, and the black folder icon [⬛] indicates a group that is closed. You can click these icons to open or close the group.

8   Hover over the Laptop Body model in the Scene panel, and click the right-pointing arrow icon [>] displayed to the right of the words "Laptop Body." This displays a new view in the Scene panel that shows you the material that is applied to the Laptop Body model.

9 With Frame Material selected, examine the Properties panel, and note that the surface properties are set up for a realistic-looking gray metallic finish on the laptop body. (You could of course change this surface to any material you wish.)

10 Click the back arrow ⬅ in the Scene panel to return to viewing the models in the panel.

11 Hover over the Glass model in the Scene panel, and click the right-pointing arrow icon ❭ displayed to the right of the word "Glass." This displays a new view in the Scene panel that shows you the material that is applied to the Glass model.

12 Examine the Properties panel, and note that the Translucence properties are set up for a glass appearance on the screen.

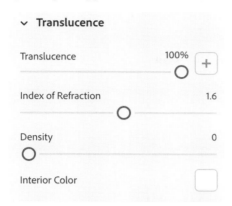

▶ **Tip:** When you are viewing a material in the Scene panel, press the Esc key to return to the list of models.

13 Click the back arrow icon ⬅ in the Scene panel to return to viewing the models in the panel.

The starter assets have easily identifiable and clearly named groups, models, and pre-applied materials, making the assets easy to work with.

Modifying a starter asset

One big advantage of a model that is made up of a group of clearly labeled sub-models is that the submodels can be transformed just like you would transform the group. This makes it easy to rotate the screen in the laptop model, "opening" or "closing" it.

1 In the Scene panel, select the Keyboard model.

2 Hold down the Shift key and then click the Laptop Body model to select the Keyboard, Trackpad Frame, and Laptop Body models.

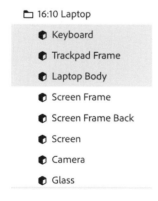

Tip: Just as with most other Adobe design applications, Command+G (macOS) or Ctrl+G (Windows) is the keyboard shortcut for Group, and Shift+Command+G (macOS) or Shift+Ctrl+G (Windows) is the keyboard shortcut for Ungroup.

3 Choose Object > Group to group the three models into a single group.

4 Double-click the name of the group to edit it, and name it **Body**.

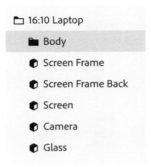

5 In the Scene panel, select the Screen Frame model.

6 Hold down the Shift key and then click the Glass model to select the Screen Frame, Screen Frame Back, Screen, Camera, and Glass models.

7 Choose Object > Group to group the five models into a single group.

8 Double-click the name of the group to edit it, and name it **Screen**.

9 Select the Select tool (keyboard shortcut: V).

10 Click the Screen group in the Scene panel to select the models that make up the laptop screen.

11 In the Properties panel, select Bottom Center for the Pivot.

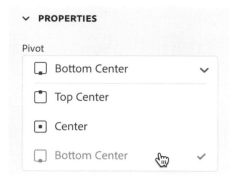

12 Drag the red circle on the Select tool widget until about 70° is displayed for the X rotation value.

● **Note:** Some 3D modeling programs allow the user to create "rigged" models. These models contain "knowledge" of how the model parts fit together. A rigged model of a laptop, for example, would allow the user to hinge the laptop screen open and closed, but not detach it from the laptop base or slide it forward or back. Dimension ignores any rigging instructions that may be present in a 3D model.

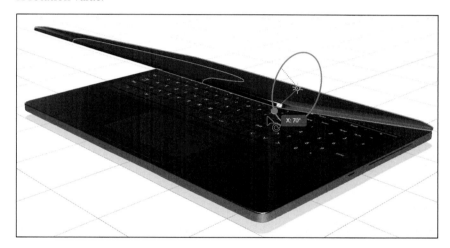

Using Adobe Stock assets

Adobe Stock is a huge collection of royalty-free images, video, artwork, templates, and 3D assets, including models, materials, and lights. These assets can be accessed through a web browser at stock.adobe.com or from within most Creative Cloud applications. The assets can be purchased via a subscription plan. See stock.adobe.com/plans for pricing information.

Finding a model on Adobe Stock

● **Note:** Just like the models that come with Dimension as starter assets, all the 3D assets available on Adobe Stock are carefully optimized for use with Dimension—they will import into a scene at a reliable size, arrive at consistent coordinates in the scene, and feature clearly named models, groups, and materials.

Several hundred of the 3D models on Adobe Stock are free, so you can use them even without an Adobe Stock subscription.

1 Click the Add And Import Content icon ⊕ at the top of the Tools panel.

2 Select Adobe Stock.

3 Select Browse all Adobe Stock 3D.

   Your default browser launches, and you are brought to a page on stock.adobe.com.

4 In your browser on the Adobe Stock page, type **182469767** into the search field at the top of the screen and then press Return/Enter.

   This is the ID number of a specific desk model used in this lesson. This model is free.

5 Click the License For Free button. If you aren't signed in to Adobe Stock with your Adobe ID, you'll be prompted for your Adobe ID and password. The asset will be licensed, and downloaded to your browser's download location.

Importing a downloaded Adobe Stock asset

Models that you license from Adobe Stock are downloaded to your browser's default download location on your computer. From there, you can import them into your Dimension scenes.

▶ **Tip:** Use the ` keyboard shortcut to show and hide the Content panel as needed to make more room on the screen for the canvas.

1 In Dimension, choose File > Import > 3D Model.

2 Navigate to your browser's default download location, open the folder named AdobeStock_182469767, select the file named a_desk_1_163.obj, and click Open. The model will be placed in the center of the scene.

3 Choose Camera > Frame All to position the camera so that you can see the entire desk on the canvas.

4 Click the Camera Bookmarks icon  at the top of the screen.

5 Click the plus icon ⊞ to create a new bookmark.

6 To rename the bookmark, type **Starting view** and press Return/Enter.

Modifying the scene

All the 3D models in the Adobe Stock library are optimized for use with Dimension, much like the starter assets. Note that the desk arrived accurately in the scene, just as the laptop did. It is centered on the scene, sized proportionally to the laptop, and sitting on the ground plane.

1 Select the Select tool (keyboard shortcut: V).

2 Click 16:10 Laptop in the Scene panel to select the laptop model.

3 Drag the green arrow up until the laptop model is floating above the top surface of the desk.

4   Select the Orbit tool (keyboard shortcut: 1) and drag down a bit on the screen so you can see more of the top of the desk.

5   Choose Camera > Frame All to position the camera so that you can see the desk and the laptop.

6   With the Select tool, drag the "Pivot Handle" (the black and white circle located on the Select tool widget on the laptop model) down to the desktop. Dragging the pivot handle snaps the model you are dragging onto the surface of any model it comes in contact with. Drag the laptop around on the surface of the desk, and position it somewhere on the left side.

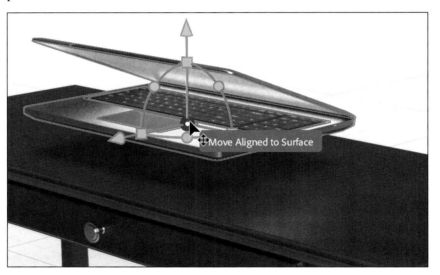

7   Drag the green circle on the Select tool widget to the right so that the laptop is turned a bit on the surface of the desk.

Adding more objects to the scene

In this lesson you'll add three more free models from Adobe Stock to your scene.

1   Click the Add And Import Content icon 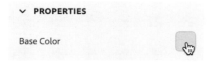 at the top of the Tools panel.

2   Select Adobe Stock, and then select Browse All Adobe Stock 3D.

3   In your browser on the Adobe Stock page, type **172516470** into the search field at the top of the screen and then press Return/Enter.

This is the ID number of a specific coffee cup model used in this lesson. This model is free.

4   Click the License For Free button. The asset will be licensed, and downloaded to your browser's download location.

5   In Dimension, choose File > Import > 3D Model.

6   Navigate to your browser's default download location, open the folder named AdobeStock_172516470, select the file named coffee_cup_116c.obj, and click Open. The model will be added to the center of the scene, and positioned on the ground plane, which in this scene is the floor beneath the desk.

7   With the Select tool, drag the "Pivot Handle" (the black and white circle located on the Select tool widget on the coffee cup) to snap the cup to the top surface of the desk. Position it anywhere you wish on the desktop,

▶ **Tip:** Two camera commands that you might find useful while positioning this small object in the larger scene are Camera > Frame Selection, which will fill the screen with the selected object, and Camera > Frame All, which will fill the screen with all the objects in the scene.

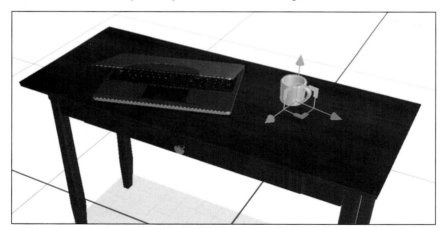

8   With the Select tool, double-click on the coffee cup model on the canvas. This will select the cup's material.

9   In the Properties panel, click the color swatch next to Base Color.

∨ **PROPERTIES**

Base Color

10 Select a blue color for the coffee cup, and then press the Esc key to close the color picker.

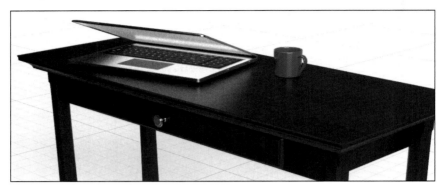

▶ **Tip:** You can also drag and drop models directly from the Finder (macOS) or File Explorer (Windows) into your scene.

11 Repeat steps 1–6, this time with Adobe Stock asset 213242110. This is the ID number of a specific composition notebook model. This model is free.

12 With the Select tool, drag the "Pivot Handle" (the black and white circle located on the Select tool widget on the composition notebook) to snap the notebook to the top surface of the desk. Position it anywhere you wish on the desktop.

13 Repeat steps 1–6 again, this time with Adobe Stock asset 184479705. This is the ID number of a wood chair model. This model is free.

14 Drag the green circle on the Select tool widget clockwise to rotate the chair so it faces the front of the desk.

15 Grab the chair, and drag it into position. Dragging a model by the body of the model, not on the Select tool widget, allows you to move the model in both directions along the ground plane, which in this case is like sliding the chair around on the floor.

Importing 3D models from other sources

In addition to working with starter assets and content from Adobe Stock, Dimension will import 3D models in the following formats:

- FBX (Filmbox)
- glTF (GL Transmission Format)
- GLB (Single-file binary version of the glTF format)
- OBJ (Wavefront)
- SKP (SketchUp)
- STL (Stereolithography)

Depending on the skill of the person who created the model and the software used, 3D models can be large and complex. In addition, different 3D modeling programs save their 3D objects into these "standard" file formats in various ways. How successful you'll be importing a model in one of these formats, and how useable the resulting model will be, depends on these variables:

- How well the modeler has created the model. For example, if the model is of a wine bottle, did the modeler create the cork in the bottle as a separate object, so that you can apply a different surface to the cork than to the rest of the bottle, or is the entire bottle a single object? Is the model constructed of enough polygons so that the curve of the bottle appears smooth, but not so many polygons that the model is overly complex?

- The model geometry. Dimension only supports polygon geometry. Alternatives to polygon modeling such as NURBs or curves aren't supported and can't be imported.

- How complex the model is relative to the processing power and memory available on your computer. For best results, a model should use the lowest number of polygons to achieve the desired appearance. The import of a model with a high polygon count may be perfectly accurate, but slow. Because the model is so complex, Dimension may subsequently be slow and unresponsive.

- How well Adobe has written the translation routine being used to translate the file format into Dimension's file format.

- How accurately, consistently, and reliably the modeling software being used writes its data into the given file format.

Unfortunately, it is nearly impossible to predict how successfully a particular model will import into Dimension. You will need to try importing it to find out! If you have a model in one of Dimension's supported formats that doesn't import properly, report the issue via the Adobe Dimension feedback website, at https://feedback.adobedimension.com.

Importing a GLB model

Most people have some personal effects, tchotchkes, or toys on their desks. You'll add a toy model of a radar antenna to the surface of the desktop.

1   In Dimension, choose File > Import > 3D Model.

▶ **Tip:** The keyboard shortcut for File > Import > 3D Model is Command+I (macOS) and Ctrl+I (Windows).

2   Select the file named DSN_34M_BWG.glb, which is in the Lessons > Lesson05 folder that you copied onto your hard disk.

3   When it comes into the scene, the model is enormous compared to the desk model. It is obviously at an entirely different scale than expected. No worries. The first step is to choose Camera > Frame Selection so that you can see the entire model.

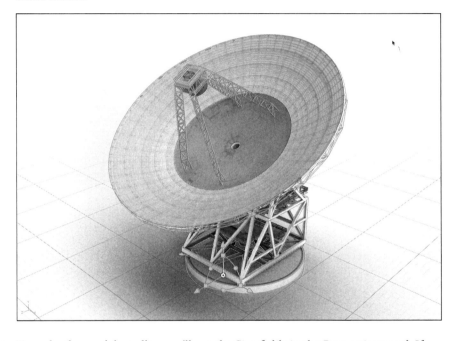

Note: The antenna model is from the repository of free 3D models available from NASA at https://solarsystem.nasa.gov/resources.

4   To make the model smaller, you'll use the Size fields in the Properties panel. If the lock icon next to Size appears unlocked 🔓, click the icon to lock the X, Y, and Z fields together so you can scale the model proportionally.

5   Enter **20 cm** for the X value, and press Return/Enter.

Size ⌄ 🔒

X 20 cm Y 21.08 cm Z 17.1 cm

6 Choose Camera > Frame All so that you can see all the models in the scene.

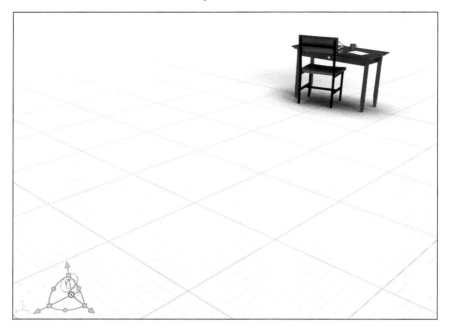

7 Now the antenna model is positioned below the ground plane. Choose Object > Move To Ground to correct this.

8 Drag the blue arrow on the Select tool widget to move the antenna closer to the desk.

9 Choose Camera > Frame All.

10 Use the Pivot Handle on the Select tool widget to position the Antenna model on the desktop as desired.

Using 3D models from Photoshop in Dimension

Photoshop can extrude text and other vector shapes into 3D space. If you want to try this for yourself, see "Creating extruded text in Photoshop" on the next page. Otherwise, I've created a PSD file ready for you to export.

1 In Adobe Photoshop, open the file named 3D text.psd, which is in the Lessons > Lesson05 folder that you copied onto your hard disk.

2 Choose 3D > Export 3D Layer.

3 Choose Wavefront|OBJ for the 3D File Format and then click OK.

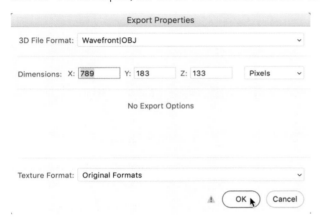

4 Type **3D text.obj** for the file name and save it somewhere you'll remember.

5 In Dimension, choose File > Import > 3D Model.

6 Navigate to where you saved the 3D text, select the file named 3D text.obj, and click Open. The model will be added to the scene, but it will be huge compared to the desk.

7 Choose Camera > Frame All.

8 To make the model smaller, you'll use the Size fields in the Properties panel. If the lock icon next to Size appears unlocked 🔓, click the icon to lock the X, Y, and Z fields together so you can scale the model proportionally.

9 Enter **30 cm** for the X value, and press Return/Enter.

10 Choose Camera > Frame All.

11 With the Select tool, drag the "Pivot Handle" (the black and white circle located on the Select tool widget on the text model) to snap the text model to the top surface of the desk. Position it anywhere you wish on the desktop,

12 Use the Camera tools (Orbit, Pan, Dolly, and Horizon) to position the camera however you want on the scene.

13 Click the Render tab, and render the scene if you wish. If you'd rather examine the render of my completed scene, open the Lesson_05_end_render.psd file in Photoshop.

Creating extruded text in Photoshop

You can use Photoshop to create extruded text and other 3D models for use in Dimension. Here are the general steps to get you started.

1 In Photoshop, create a new document that is 1000 px x 1000 px.

2 With the Type tool, create a single word or line of type.

3 Make the text large.

4 Choose 3D > New 3D Extrusion from Selected Layer.

5 If you are asked if you want to switch to the 3D workspace, click Yes.

6 Use the Properties panel to experiment with Shape Preset, Extrusion Depth, and other settings.

Other sources for 3D content

There are dozens of websites that sell stock 3D content. Because of the complexity of 3D models and file formats, it's important that you purchase models from reputable vendors that will stand behind their product if the models won't import into Dimension.

Here is a sampling of some stock 3D sources:

- CGTrader: cgtrader.com
- Sketchfab: sketchfab.com/store
- Turbosquid: www.turbosquid.com

There are also various repositories of free 3D content on the web. Here are a few:

- 3D Warehouse: 3dwarehouse.sketchup.com
- Google Poly: poly.google.com
- GrabCAD: grabcad.com
- National Institutes of Health: 3dprint.nih.gov
- Smithsonian: 3d.si.edu
- Traceparts: traceparts.com

Identifying potential problems when importing 3D models

Models that you place in your scene from the starter assets or from Adobe Stock should import into Dimension in a reliable, consistent manner. But models you obtain from other sources may sometimes behave unpredictably when imported into Dimension. Here are some of the potential problems, as well as a few solutions.

Model appears out of scale

The creator of a model doesn't have any idea of the size at which you want to use the model, so it may come into Dimension enormous or really tiny. If the problem isn't too extreme, you can scale the object with the Select tool. Or use the Dolly tool (keyboard shortcut: 3) to enlarge or reduce your view of the object.

Sometimes, an object will arrive so large that just a single small surface on the object fills the entire screen, so it is difficult to scale the object or zoom in or out. In this case, the Camera > Frame Selection command (keyboard shortcut: F) will scale your view so that the entire object fits on the screen.

Object positioned outside the viewable area

Sometimes an object won't appear anywhere within the Dimension window. This is caused by the XYZ positioning of the object being out of scale with Dimension's coordinate system. Thankfully, when this happens, a blue dot icon ⬤ will appear at the edge of the screen. Clicking this icon will position the screen so that you can see the imported object.

Object positioned below the ground plane

Sometimes an object won't appear on the screen because it is entirely below the ground plane. Choosing Object > Move to Ground will quickly move the object above the ground plane so that it is within view.

Review questions

1 Which of these file formats can be imported as a 3D model into a Dimension scene?

PSD

OBJ

MTL

CAN

2 Are 3D models in the Adobe Stock library free or paid?

3 What does the Object > Move To Ground command do, and when might you need to use it?

4 If an imported model is much larger than the canvas, what is one easy way to quickly position the camera so that you can see the entire model?

Review answers

1 OBJ is an industry-standard 3D file format that can be exported from many different 3D modeling programs and placed into a Dimension scene.

2 The 3D models available in the Adobe Stock library can be purchased via a monthly subscription. However, several hundred of the 3D models on Adobe Stock are free.

3 The Object > Move To Ground command will move the selected object so that it is positioned above the ground plane. This command is sometimes necessary when an imported model doesn't appear within view because it is positioned "underground," beneath the ground plane.

4 The Camera > Frame Selection command (keyboard shortcut: F) will quickly position the camera so that the entire model is within view.

6 WORKING WITH MATERIALS

Lesson overview

In this lesson, you'll explore and apply surface materials in a 3D scene and learn the following:

- An overview of the types of materials included with Dimension.

- How to import materials from Adobe Stock.

- How to import materials from other sources.

- How to select model surfaces with the Magic Wand tool and then apply materials to those surfaces.

- How to adjust material properties, such as glow, opacity, and translucence.

- How materials can be linked between multiple models.

This lesson will take about 45 minutes to complete. To get the lesson files used in this chapter, download them from the web page for this book at www.adobepress.com/DimensionCIB2020. For more information, see "Accessing the lesson files and Web Edition" in the Getting Started section at the beginning of this book.

You can apply infinite variations of surface materials to models in Dimension, including metals, glass, plastic, wood, fabrics, and more.

What are materials?

One of the core capabilities of Dimension is the ability to apply a "material" to a 3D object. Materials are usually carefully crafted to accurately simulate materials found in the physical world, such as tile, marble, granite, wood, or fabric.

Dimension can apply two types of materials to models: Adobe Standard Materials (MDL format) and Substances (SBSAR format). The MDL format is a subset of the NVidia Material Definition Language that Adobe calls Adobe Standard Material. This format defines how light behaves when it hits the surface of the material. For example, is light emitted from the surface? If so, how much? Is the surface opaque, transparent, or semi-transparent? Is the surface rough or smooth? Does the surface exhibit "luster" like shiny metal? If you can see through the object to the interior, is the interior translucent, and does the object refract the light?

▶ **Tip:** You can read more about Adobe Standard Material at helpx.adobe.com/ dimension/using/ standard-materials.html.

MDL materials can optionally include images that can control properties of the material. For example, a brick material may include a color image for the variations of brick color, a roughness image to give areas shiny or matte effects, and a "normal" image that adds details like pores to the surface.

SBSAR materials originate in Substance Designer. Adobe purchased Allegorithmic, the parent company of Substance Designer, in early 2019. The speciality of Substance Designer is creating parametrically-generated materials, or materials that can be dynamically controlled by one or more parameters. For example, a parametric SBSAR concrete material may allow the user to dynamically control the number of cracks in the concrete, the width of the cracks, variations in the color of the concrete, and the roughness of the surface. From a single parametric material, a user can create an infinite variety of random surface variations.

▶ **Tip:** Learn more about the Substance family of products at www.substance3d.com.

This lesson is a deep dive into materials. Another way to change the appearance of a model's surface is to apply one or more graphic images to the surface. Any JPEG, PNG, AI, PSD, or SVG file can be applied to a model surface as an image. Applying graphics to model surfaces is covered in depth in a later lesson.

Finding materials

Several dozen starter asset materials can be found in Dimension's Assets panel, including several types of glass, metals, plastics, liquids, woods, papers, leathers, stones, and fabrics. You can also download hundreds of additional materials from Adobe Stock or obtain MDL and SBSAR files from other sources and place them on your models in Dimension.

1 Choose File > Open.

2 Select the file named Lesson_06_01_begin.dn, which is in the Lessons > Lesson06 folder that you copied onto your hard disk, and then click Open.

3 Click the Add And Import Content icon ⊕ at the top of the Tools panel, and choose Starter Assets.

4 Click the Materials icon to view only materials in the panel.

5 Click the more icon to toggle between list view and grid view until the materials are displayed in the way that you prefer. Scroll through the panel and note the many different types of starter materials available. Note that the materials are grouped by type, with Adobe Standard Materials at the top of the list and Substance Materials at the bottom. As you'll see in this lesson, you can change the properties of each of these materials, so these are a good starting point for generating a wide variety of surface materials.

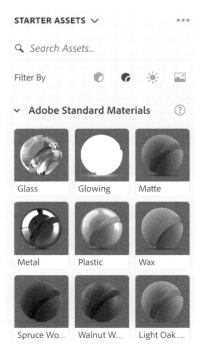

6   Scroll to the bottom of the list of starter materials, and click the words "Browse Adobe Stock."

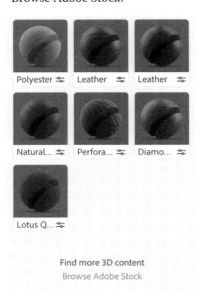

Find more 3D content
Browse Adobe Stock

▶ **Tip:** To place an MDL or SBSAR material that you download , choose File > Import > Place Material On Selection.

Your default web browser launches, and you're taken to stock.adobe.com, where you'll see hundreds of additional materials available for purchase.

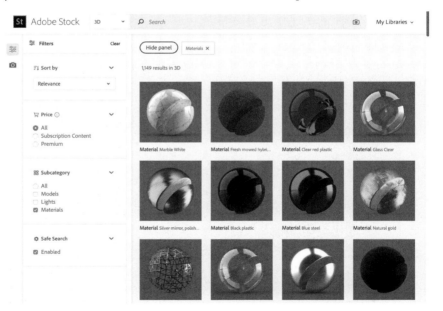

Sources for SBSAR materials

If you purchase a Substance license at www.substance3d.com, you'll have access to Substance Designer, which lets you create your own SBSAR materials. A license also gives you access to download professionally-designed materials on Substance Source at source.substance3d.com.

A Substance license is not needed to download free community-submitted materials from Substance Share at share.substance3d.com. Since these are free community-created assets, the quality varies. For compatibility with Dimension, sort the materials by release date, since some of the very old SBSAR materials won't work in Dimension.

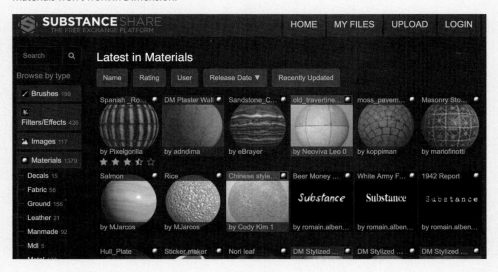

Applying a material to an object

In this lesson, you're going to apply various materials from the Starter Assets to models in this scene.

1   Select the Select tool (keyboard shortcut: V).

2   Select Cup 2 in the Scene panel to select the cup that is lying on its side.

3   In the Search Assets field at the top of the Starter Assets panel, type **plastic**.

4   Select the Plastic MDL material to apply it to the cup.

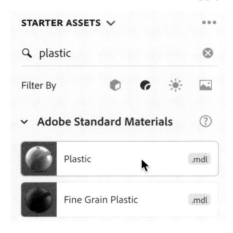

5   If you aren't currently working with Render Preview on, click the Render Preview icon ▦ to turn it on. Materials preview much more accurately with Render Preview on.

6   Examine the Scene panel. The Scene panel confirms that the Plastic material has been applied to the Cup 2 model.

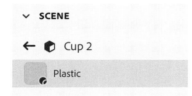

> **Tip:** As an alternative to clicking the back arrow at the top of the Scene panel, you can press the Esc key to "back up" out of the materials view in the Scene panel and return to the model list.

7   Click the back arrow icon ← at the top of the Scene panel to return to the model list.

8   Select Cup 3 in the Scene panel to select the rightmost cup.

9 In the Search Assets field at the top of the Assets panel, type **glass**.

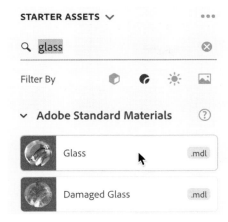

10 Select the Glass MDL material to apply it to the cup.

Applying materials via drag and drop

Sometimes it's more convenient to apply a material to a model by dragging the material from the Starter Assets, from a Library, or from your file system onto the surface of a model.

1 Choose Edit > Deselect All so that none of the objects in the scene are selected.

2 In the Search Assets field at the top of the Assets panel, type **metal**.

3 Drag the Metal material onto the leftmost cup in the scene. Release the mouse button when you see a blue highlight around the cup.

4   Click the back arrow icon ← at the top of the Scene panel (or press Esc) to return to the model list.

5   The Twist Jar object is a group, as indicated by the Group icon ▣ in the Scene panel. Click the Group icon to open the group. You'll see that the group consists of two models: Lid and Jar. Because this object was modeled as two separate models, you can easily apply separate materials to the lid and the jar. Note that you can open a group without selecting the group. If you accidentally select the Twist Jar group, choose Edit > Deselect All.

6   In the Assets panel, locate the Geometric Metal SBSAR material and drag it onto the Twist Jar model in the scene. Release the mouse button when you see a blue highlight around the jar body (not the lid).

Sampling a material from another model

Once you've applied a material to a model, you can easily apply the same material to other models with the Sampler tool.

1   Click the back arrow icon ← at the top of the Scene panel (or press Esc) to return to the model list.

2   In the Scene panel, select the Lid model under Twist Jar.

3   In the Tools panel, select the Sampler tool (keyboard shortcut: I).

4   Right-click the Sampler tool, and verify that Sample Type is set to Material since
    you want to sample all the material attributes, not just the material color.

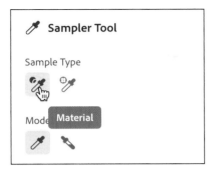

5   Click away from the Sampler tool options box to dismiss the box.

6   Click anywhere on the middle cup on the canvas (the plastic cup lying on its
    side). This will sample the Plastic material from the cup model and apply it to
    what you have selected (the lid of the small jar).

Changing MDL material properties

So far, you've applied starter asset materials without setting any of their properties.
But every material can be customized in several ways using the Properties panel.

1   Click the back arrow icon ← at the top of the Scene panel (or press Esc) to
    return to the model list.

2   In the Scene panel, hover over the Cup 2 model, and click the right arrow
    icon > to reveal the model materials.

3 To make the plastic material a bright orange, click the color swatch next to the base color in the Properties panel, and change the color to **255** red, **123** green, **0** blue.

▶ Tip: If you hover over a property name in the Properties panel, a question mark will appear. If you click the property name, you'll see an animated visual explanation of what that property does.

4 Click the color swatch again to close the color picker.

5 To make the surface a bit shinier, in the Properties panel, increase the Metallic value to **10%**.

Because the material for the Jar Lid model was sampled from the Cup 2 model, both models use the same Plastic material, so both are now orange and shiny. Changing the properties of the material on one object also changes the properties of the material on the other object. But what if you want the Cup 2 model to be rougher and less metallic than the Jar Lid? You can achieve this by unlinking the material between the two models.

6   Select the Break Link To Material icon  in the Actions panel. Now the materials on the two models are unlinked and their properties can be manipulated independently.

7   With the Cup 2 plastic material still selected in the Scene panel, enter **25%** for the Roughness value.

8   Enter **0%** for the Metallic property.

9   Click the back arrow icon ← at the top of the Scene panel (or press Esc) to return to the model list.

10 Hover over Cup 1 in the Scene panel, and click the right arrow icon ▷ to reveal the model materials.

11 To make the surface a bright orange, in the Properties panel, click the color swatch next to the base color, and change the color to **255** red, **123** green, **0** blue.

12 Click the color swatch again to close the color picker.

13 To make the surface less reflective, increase the Roughness value to **30%**.

14 Click the plus icon ⊞ to the right of the Roughness slider.

15 Click Select a File.

16 Select the Dots-white.png file and click Open.

With this PNG mask applied, areas that are black in the PNG will be smooth metallic in the image, and white areas will be rough.

Tip: Double-clicking a model on the canvas will reveal the model's materials in the Scene panel. This is an alternative to clicking the right arrow icon in the Scene panel.

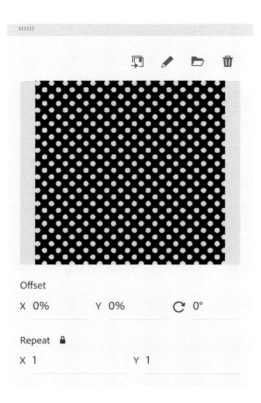

Offset

X 0%   Y 0%   ↻ 0°

Repeat 🔒

X 1   Y 1

▶ **Tip:** You can greatly speed up the Render Preview by hiding models you don't need to preview. To hide a model, click the eye icon 👁 next to a model in the Scene panel.

17 Press the Esc key to close the image picker and return to the model list in the Scene panel.

How bitmap images affect material properties

If you examine the Properties panel when an MDL material applied to a model is selected, you'll see that you can add a bitmap image to the Opacity, Roughness, Metallic, Glow, and Translucence properties to alter the ways these properties behave.

- When a bitmap image is added to Opacity, black areas are transparent and white areas are opaque.

- When a bitmap image is added to Roughness, black areas are polished and white areas are matte.

- When a bitmap image is added to Metallic, black areas are non-metallic and white areas are metallic.

- When a bitmap image is added to Glow, black areas reflect light and white areas emit light.

- When a bitmap image is added to Translucence, black areas are non-translucent and white areas are translucent.

Changing MDL glass material properties

Adjusting the Translucence properties of a material makes it appear like glass or liquid—you can see through it. You can alter the Translucence, Index of Refraction, Density, and Interior Color properties in the Properties panel to make models appear to be made of glass, liquid, or gel.

1 Hover over the Cup 3 model in the Scene panel, and click the right arrow icon > to reveal the model materials.

2 If the Translucence properties aren't already open, in the Properties panel, click the right arrow icon > next to Translucence to reveal them.

3 To make the glass more "foggy" or "cloudy," enter a Translucence value of **90%**.

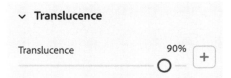

4   To cause the glass to "bend," or refract the light more, enter **2.8** for the Index of Refraction. You won't see the effect of this unless you have Render Preview turned on.

Index of Refraction   2.8

5   Click the back arrow ⬅ at the top of the Scene panel to return to the model list.

Changing SBSAR material properties

1   If the Twist Jar group isn't open, click its Group icon 📁 to open it.

2   Hover over the Jar model (not the lid), and click the right arrow icon ➤ to reveal the model materials.

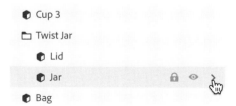

3 Since Geometric Metal is a parametric SBSAR material, there are numerous adjustable parameters defined by the material creator. To start, enter **2.1** for both the X and Y Repeat.

4 Experiment with the rest of the parameters in the Properties panel. I used Wind Shim Embossed for the Pattern Selection, **.27** for the Rotation, **.73** for the Gap, and **1.6** for the Bevel, and left the rest of the values as-is.

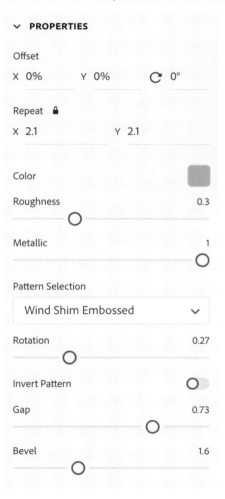

Sub-selecting model faces

You've seen that models can consist of a group of sub-models. When an object is modeled this way, it is easy to select the various sub-model components independently. Sometimes you may find that you want to apply different materials to different "parts" of a model, but although they look like separate parts, they weren't created as separate sub-models.

Assuming that the parts in question look different from the surrounding surfaces on the model, there is a way to apply different materials to different surfaces on a single model. The key is to use the Magic Wand tool. The Magic Wand tool works similarly to the Magic Wand tool in Photoshop. When you click a surface with the Magic Wand, Dimension attempts to select the surface up to its "edges." Let's try it out.

1   Double-click the Magic Wand tool.

2   Set the Selection Size to Tiny.

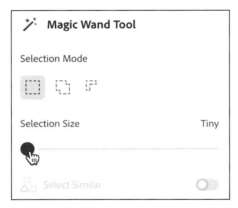

3   Click inside the cup that is on its side on the table. Note that a blue selection boundary appears around the inside area of the cup.

4   In the Content panel, type **plastic** into the search field.

5   Select the Plastic MDL material to apply the white plastic material to the inside surface of the cup.

6   In the Scene panel, hover over Cup 2 and click the right arrow icon to reveal the model materials.

Note that now Cup 2 has two materials applied: Plastic and Plastic 3. (Depending on what you've done previously, your second plastic material might be followed by a numeral other than 3).

7   Click the back arrow ← at the top of the Scene panel to return to the model list.

Applying materials to the star

Although the Star model in our scene consists of a single model, you can use the Magic Wand tool to select just some of the surfaces of the star and apply different materials to these surfaces.

1   Select the Star model in the Scene panel.

2   Choose Camera > Frame Selection to position the camera to give a large view of the Star model.

3   In the Content panel, type **cardboard** into the search field.

4 Select the Cardboard SBSAR material to apply it to the star.

5 Click one of the triangular "sides" of the star with the Magic Wand tool. You'll see the triangle highlighted in blue to indicate it is selected.

6 Hold down the Shift key, and click every other facet of the star face. Holding down the Shift key lets you add to the selection each time you click with the Magic Wand tool.

7 In the Content panel, type **paper** into the search field.

8 Select the Diagonal Paper SBSAR material to apply it to the star facets.

9 In the Scene panel, hover over "Star" and click the right arrow icon 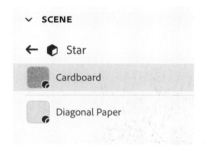 to reveal the model materials.

Note that now the Star model has two materials applied: Cardboard and Diagonal Paper.

10 Click the Camera Bookmarks icon and select Final view to return to the original camera view.

Applying materials to the bag

1 Double-click the Magic Wand tool (keyboard shortcut: W).

2 Change the Selection size to medium.

3 Click on the front of the body of the bag (not the handles).

4 In the Content panel, type **plastic** into the search field.

5 Select the Plastic With Lattice Pattern MDL material to apply it to the bag.

6 If you have time, render the scene. Or open and examine the Lesson_06_01_end_render_high.psd file, which I've rendered for you.

Linking and unlinking materials

In the preceding example, you sampled the material for the Jar Lid model from the Cup 2 model. This created a single material instance that was linked between both models. When you changed the material color, it was updated on both models. As noted, you can unlink the material if you want to control the attributes of the material on each object independently.

Dimension follows a fairly subtle set of rules as to when it links materials and when it doesn't. Let's examine material linking more closely and see how Dimension decides when to link materials.

Applying materials en masse

You can apply materials to several models at the same time, resulting in a common linked material, which makes quick work of altering those models.

1 Choose File > Open.

2 Select the file named Lesson_06_02_begin.dn, which is in the Lessons > Lesson06 folder that you copied onto your hard disk, and then click Open.

3 Select the Select tool (keyboard shortcut: V).

4 Select all three sphere models: click one of the models, hold down the Shift key, and click each of the other two models. Notice that the spheres aren't grouped together.

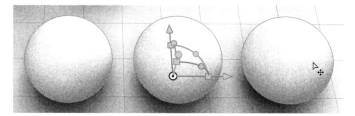

5 In the Content panel, select the Plastic MDL material to apply it to the three selected spheres all at once. When you apply a material to multiple objects with a single click, the material is linked between the objects by default.

6 Choose Edit > Deselect All to deselect the sphere models.

7 In the Scene panel, hover over the Sphere 1 model, and click the right arrow icon > | to reveal the material applied to the sphere.

You will see a Break Link To Material icon [icon] appear in the Actions panel. The presence of this icon tells you that the material you have selected is linked to at least one other model.

8   In the Properties panel, click the color swatch next to Base Color, and change the color to a bright red. The material color of all three spheres changes because all three models share a common linked material. **Conclusion: when you apply a material to multiple objects with a single click, the material is linked between the objects by default.**

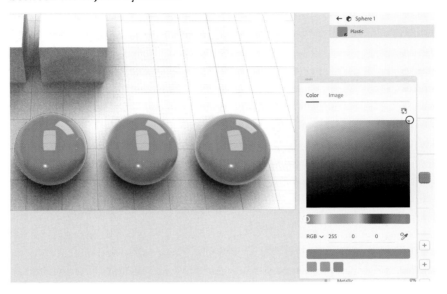

Breaking a link

When you no longer want the material that is applied to multiple models to be linked, you can break the link, allowing you to individually modify the material applied to the models.

1   Click the back arrow icon ⬅ at the top of the Scene panel to return to the model list.

2   Hover over the Sphere 2 model, and click the right arrow icon ➤ to reveal the material applied to the sphere.

3   Click the Break Link To Material icon ⟲ in the Actions panel. The icon will disappear from the Actions panel, indicating that the material is no longer linked to another model.

4   In the Properties panel, click the color swatch next to Base Color, and change the color to a bright green.

    The material of Sphere 2 is the only one to change color, since it contains an independent material that is no longer linked to the other spheres.

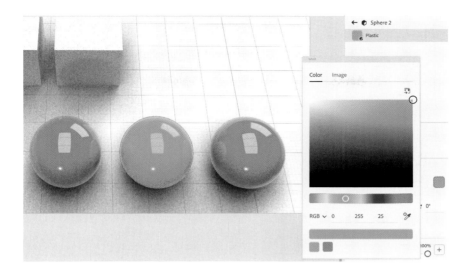

Applying materials one at a time

If you apply the same material to several objects one at a time, the material is not linked between the models. The material applied to each model is a separate "instance" of the material. The properties of the material instance can be changed without affecting the other models.

1 Choose Edit > Deselect All.

2 Locate the Matte MDL material in the Content panel, and drag it onto the leftmost sphere model.

3 Drag the Matte material onto the middle sphere model.

4 Drag the Matte material onto the rightmost sphere model.

5 Press the Esc key to display the model list in the Scene panel.

6 Double-click the leftmost sphere to reveal the material applied to the sphere in the Scene panel.

No Break Link To Material icon  is displayed in the Actions panel. This means that the material you have selected is not linked to any other models.

7 In the Properties panel, click the color swatch next to Base Color and change the color to a bright red.

The material of Sphere 1 is the only one to change color, since it contains an independent material that is not linked to the other spheres. **Conclusion: when you apply materials independently to objects one at a time, even if you apply the same material to each model, the materials are unlinked by default.**

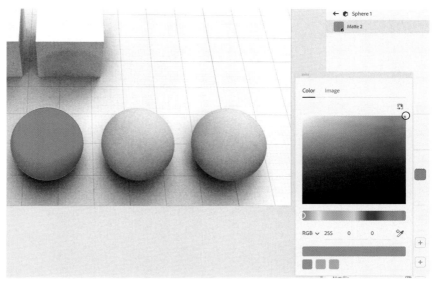

Applying materials with the Sampler tool

If you want to apply a material used on one model to another model, you can do so with the Sampler tool. The result will be a material that is linked between the two models.

1   Click the back arrow icon ⬅ at the top of the Scene panel to return to the model list.

2   In the Scene panel, click Cube 1 to select it.

3   In the Content panel, select the Metal MDL material to apply it to the surface of Cube 1.

4   Click the back arrow icon ⬅ at the top of the Scene panel to return to the model list.

5   Click Cube 2 in the Scene panel to select it.

6   Select the Sampler tool (keyboard shortcut: I), and click the Cube 1 model (the cube with the metal material applied) on the canvas.

7   The Scene panel shows that the Metal material is applied to the Cube 2 model. Note that the Break Link To Material icon 🔗 appears in the Actions panel. This is your cue that the metal material used for Cube 1 is linked to Cube 2.

8   In the Properties panel, click the color swatch next to Base Color and change the color to a bright red.

Since they are linked, the material color on both Cube 1 and Cube 2 changes. **Conclusion: when you use the Sampler tool to sample a material from one model to another, the materials in both models will be linked by default.**

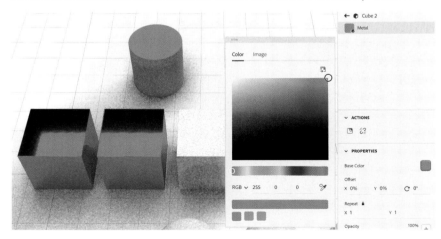

Understanding Paste vs. Paste As Instance

Dimension has two Paste commands in the Edit menu: Paste, and Paste As Instance. After you've copied a model to the clipboard, both of these commands will paste a duplicate of the model. But the two commands differ in how the material on the duplicate model is linked to that of the original model.

1   Select the Select tool (keyboard shortcut: V).

2   Select the cylinder model at the top of the scene.

3   Choose Edit > Copy.

4   Choose Edit > Paste.

5   Drag the blue arrow to the right so you can see both cylinders.

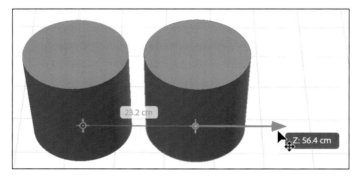

6   On the canvas, double-click the duplicate cylinder that you just created to reveal the cylinder material in the Scene panel.

7   In the Properties panel, click the color swatch next to Base Color and change the color to a bright green.

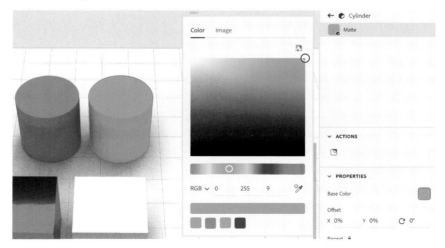

Since they aren't linked, the material on only one of the cylinders changes.
Conclusion: by default, when you copy and paste a model, use the Edit > Duplicate command, or Option/Alt-drag to duplicate a model, the materials of the models aren't linked.

8 Select the green cylinder model.

9 Choose Edit > Copy.

10 Choose Edit > Paste As Instance.

11 Drag the blue arrow to the right so you can see both green cylinders.

12 On the canvas, double-click the duplicate green cylinder that you just created to reveal the cylinder material in the Scene panel.

13 In the Properties panel, click the color swatch next to Base Color and change the color to blue.

The material color on both cylinders changes since the materials are linked.
Conclusion: when you use the Paste As Instance command, the materials in both models are linked by default.

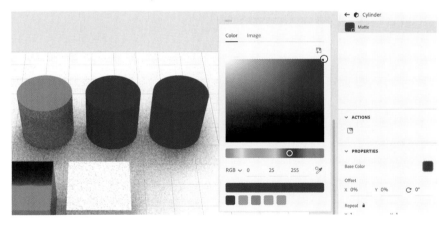

Linking summary

The subtleties of how Dimension links materials between objects can be boiled down to the following:

- When you apply a material to multiple objects with a single click, the material is linked between the objects by default.

- When you apply materials to objects one at a time, even if you apply the same material, the materials are unlinked by default.

- When you use the Sampler tool to sample a material from one model to another, the materials in both models are linked by default.

- When you copy and paste, use the Edit > Duplicate command, or Option/Alt-drag to duplicate a model, the materials of the models are not linked.

- When you copy a model and use the Paste As Instance command, the materials in both models are linked by default.

Review questions

1 What is the main difference between MDL and SBSAR materials?

2 What tool do you use to apply separate materials to different parts of a single model?

3 When using the Magic Wand tool, how do you add to a selection?

4 What tool would you use to sample a material from one model and apply it to another?

5 If you drag the same material onto five objects, one object at a time, will the same material be linked to all five objects?

Review answers

1 MDL models all offer the same group of adjustable settings, such as opacity, roughness, metallic, and translucence. SBSAR models are "parametric," meaning that they offer many different parameters depending on the whim of artist who created the material.

2 The Magic Wand tool allows you to "subselect" individual surfaces of a model and apply a different material to each surface.

3 After you've clicked with the Magic Wand tool to select a surface on a model, hold down the Shift key and click another surface to extend the selection.

4 You can use the Sampler tool (keyboard shortcut: I) to sample a material from one model and quickly apply it to another model.

5 No. If you drag the same material onto five objects, one object at a time, each object will have an independent instance of the material and not be linked to any other models. If you select all five models and apply a material to all five models at once, then the same material is linked to all five models.

7 CREATING MATERIALS WITH ADOBE CAPTURE

Lesson overview

In this lesson, you'll use the Adobe Capture mobile app and learn the following:

- How to use Capture to create unique materials to use in Adobe Dimension.

- How to edit materials in Adobe Capture to fit your needs.

- How to use materials you've created with Capture in Adobe Dimension.

 This lesson will take about 45 minutes to complete. To get the lesson files used in this chapter, download them from the web page for this book at www.adobepress.com/DimensionCIB2020. For more information, see "Accessing the lesson files and Web Edition" in the Getting Started section at the beginning of this book.

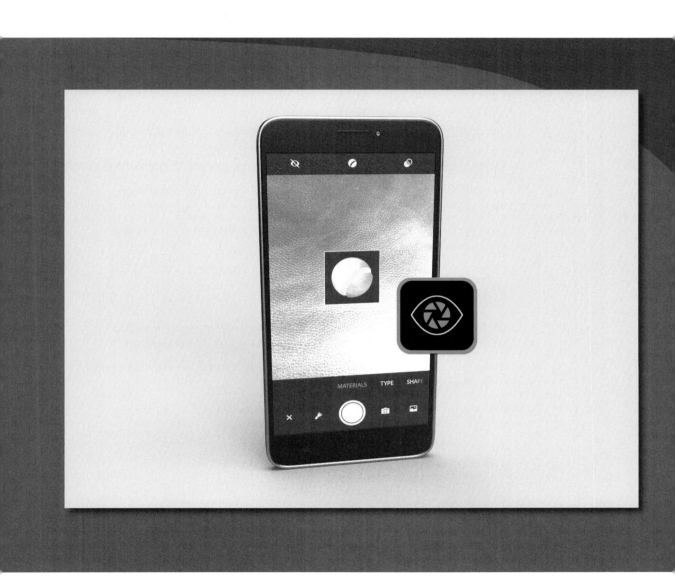

The Adobe Capture mobile app is a fun and powerful way to create interesting materials that you can apply to your models in Adobe Dimension.

About Adobe Capture

Adobe Capture is a mobile app for iOS and Android devices. The purpose of Capture is to enable you to capture inspiration from the world around you and turn that inspiration into type, brushes, patterns, shapes, colors, gradients, and—specifically for our purposes in Dimension—materials.

When you are out and about and see a material or texture that you think would work well for a model in Dimension, you can shoot a photo of the texture with your mobile device's camera and, in a few taps of the screen, turn it into a material ready to apply to a model in Dimension.

You can learn more about Adobe Capture at www.adobe.com/products/capture.html.

Download and install Adobe Capture on your mobile device

To download and install Adobe Capture on your iPhone or iPad, go to www.adobe.com/go/getcapture_ios.

To download and install Adobe Capture on your Android mobile device, visit www.adobe.com/go/getcapture_android.

Capturing a material

You can capture a material from a photo that you take with your device, from a stock photo, or from any asset you've saved in Creative Cloud. Here's how.

1   Launch Adobe Capture on your mobile device. If prompted, sign in with your Adobe ID.

2 If the Capture preferences on your device are set so that Capture opens directly into camera mode, tap the X in the lower-left corner of the screen to close the camera.

3 At the top of the screen, choose a CC Library from the menu. If you're unfamiliar with CC Libraries, just choose My Library.

4 Tap Materials at the top of the screen.

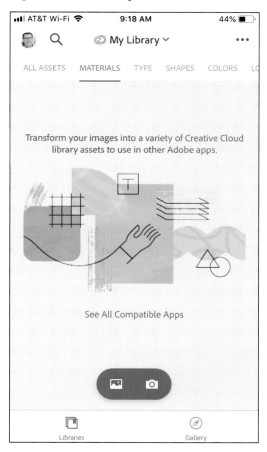

5 Tap the Camera icon .

6 Point the camera at an interesting texture or pattern, and then tap the 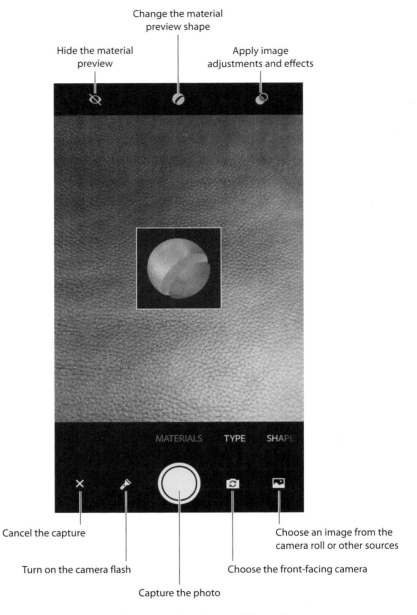 icon to take a photo.

● **Note:** You can tap the sphere in the middle of the screen at any time to freeze the view. Then, if it's available on your mobile device, you can tap the image adjustments and effects icon in the upper-right corner to adjust the exposure, color, and special effects on the image being captured.

Change the material preview shape

Hide the material preview

Apply image adjustments and effects

MATERIALS TYPE SHAPE

Cancel the capture

Choose an image from the camera roll or other sources

Turn on the camera flash

Choose the front-facing camera

Capture the photo

7 Make adjustments to the material attributes, if desired.

- Roughness controls how shiny the surface is. A higher value makes the surface rougher, allowing less shine on the surface.

- Detail controls the details in the surface. Increasing the Detail value adds detail to the surface with a sharpening effect.

- Metallic controls the degree of metallic luster on the surface. A higher value makes the surface appear more metallic.

- Increasing the Intensity setting makes the surface texture higher, and decreasing the setting makes it lower. This value affects the "normal map" bitmap image that appears in the Properties panel in Dimension when the material is applied to a model.

- Frequency determines the light and shadow. Adjusting the Frequency value adjusts the sharpening effect to the normal map, changing the appearance of light and shadow on the surface.

- Repeat changes the "tile" size of the material. A larger value results in a smaller image that will repeat more frequently when used on a large model. A smaller value will repeat less frequently.

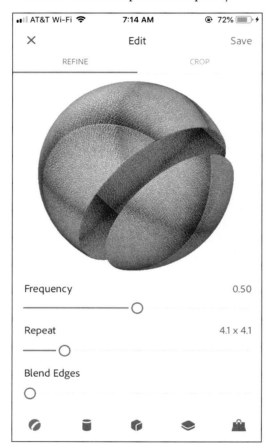

- If you increase the Blend Edges value, Capture will attempt to blend the edges between each tile when a material repeats across a model's surface.

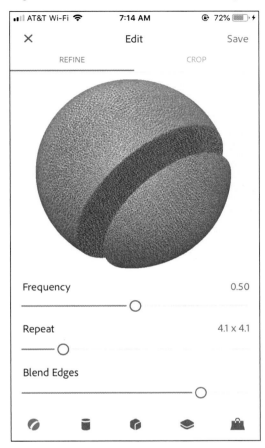

8 Tap Save to save the material. The material is added to the CC Library you chose in step 2 and is ready to use in Dimension.

Capture a material from a photo

In addition to capturing materials from your mobile device's camera, you can also capture materials from a photo that is in your device's camera roll, that you previously saved in your Creative Cloud storage, that you've brought into Lightroom, that is from Adobe Stock, or that is from any other source you have access to on your device, such as Dropbox or Google Drive.

Tip: If you want to change the name of your material, tap the More icon ••• next to the name of the material on the material thumbnails screen and tap Rename.

1 Launch Adobe Capture on your mobile device.

2 If the Capture preferences on your device are set so that Capture opens directly into camera mode, tap the X in the lower-left corner of the screen to close the camera.

3 At the top of the screen, choose a CC Library from the menu. If you're unfamiliar with CC Libraries, just choose My Library.

4 Tap Materials at the top of the screen.

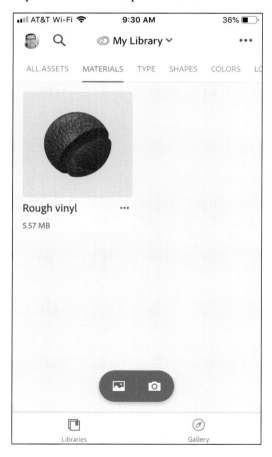

5 Tap the image icon 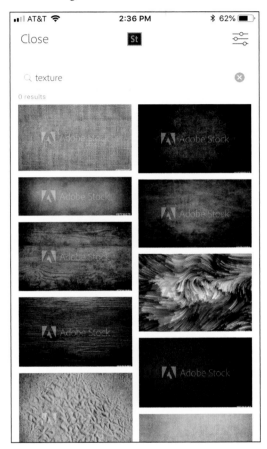.

6 Tap Stock from the pop-up list to access Adobe Stock.

7 In the search field, type **texture** and then tap Search. This will reveal hundreds of texture images.

8 Tap a texture that you like.

9 Tap either Save Preview (to download a watermarked comp image) or License Asset (to purchase the image).

10 Choose a CC Library to save the stock image to.

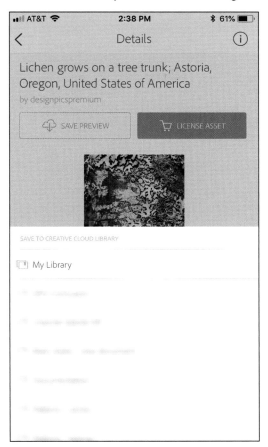

11 Tap the capture icon ◎ to bring the image into Adobe Capture.

12 Make adjustments to the material attributes, if desired.

13 Tap Save to save the material to your CC Library.

Using a material from Capture in Dimension

Applying a material that was created in Adobe Capture to a model is just like applying a material from any other source. The only difference is that you need to look for the material in a CC Library.

1 Launch Adobe Dimension.

2 Choose File > Open.

3 Select the file named Lesson_07_01_begin.dn, which is in the Lessons > Lesson07 folder that you copied onto your hard disk, and then click Open.

4 Click the Add And Import Content icon ⊕ at the top of the Tools panel, and choose CC Libraries.

5 In the menu just under the search field at the top of the Content panel, choose the library that you saved your captured materials into.

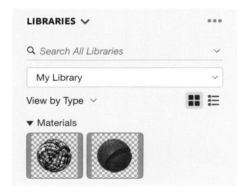

6 Drag one of the materials you created with Adobe Capture onto the Prism model on the canvas. Or, if you prefer, select the Prism model, choose File > Import > Place Material On Selection, and select the Material_14.mdl file in the Bricks folder to use the Brick material created for you with Capture.

7 Drag another one of the materials you created with Adobe Capture onto the Pipe model on the canvas. Or, if you prefer, select the Pipe model, choose File > Import > Place Material On Selection, and select the Material_6.mdl file in the Maple folder to use the Maple wood material created for you with Capture.

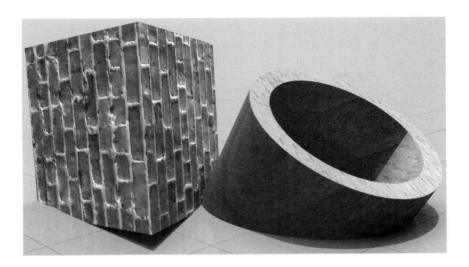

Modifying material properties

You may need to adjust several things after applying a material generated by Capture to a model in Dimension. A material created with Capture is a photographic bitmap of a specific width and height, along with other bitmaps that define the roughness, metallic luster, and texture of the material. A captured material might not be the correct size or orientation relative to your model, seams may be visible in the material, or the material may appear too smooth or too rough. Here are some ways to rectify these problems.

Material not aligned with model

1 Choose File > Open.

2 Select the file named Lesson_07_02_begin.dn, which is in the Lessons > Lesson07 folder that you copied onto your hard disk, and then click Open. If you still have Lesson_07_01_begin.dn open, you can close it without saving.

3 The scene looks strange with the bricks running vertically up and down the model. Hover over Prism in the Scene panel, and click the right arrow icon ⟩ to reveal the material applied to the prism.

4   In the Properties panel, Enter **−90°** for the rotation value to rotate the bricks to align horizontally with the prism.

Material too small or too large compared to the model

When you create a material with Capture, you won't have a sense of how large or small the pattern or texture will be relative to the model you will apply it to. You can scale the material up or down in Dimension.

1   If you no longer have the Prism material selected, double-click the Prism model on the canvas with the Select tool.

2   The bricks look a little large in the scene. In the Properties panel, enter **1.5** for the Repeat X and Y values. Entering a larger value for Repeat causes the bitmap to shrink in size and to repeat multiple times, if necessary, to cover the entire model surface. Entering a smaller value enlarges the bitmap so that any visible texture in the material becomes larger relative to the model.

Seam visible in material when applied to the model

Sometimes a seam will be visible in the material applied to a model. In this scene, the seam is quite visible on the Maple material that is applied to the pipe.

There are a couple things that can cause a seam. First, if a material is not large enough to cover the entire surface of the model, it will repeat, or "tile," across the surface of the model. When this happens, a seam will usually be visible where the material repeats.

This can usually be fixed by applying a "Blend Edges" value when creating the material in Adobe Capture, as described earlier. Or, you may be able to hide the seam by adjusting the offset or repeat values in the Properties panel.

In this scene, however, the seam is caused by the material "wrapping" around from the beginning to the end of the inside surface of the cylinder. So the only way to fix this is to rotate the pipe to hide the seam.

1   If you currently have a material selected, press the Esc key, and then select the Pipe model with the Select tool.

2   Double-click the Select tool, and make sure that Align To Scene is turned off. This is to ensure that the Pipe rotates around its tilted axis, not around a vertical axis.

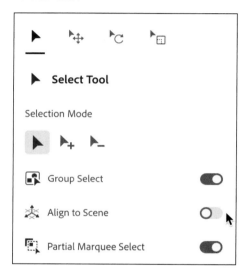

3   Drag the green circle on the transformation widget to the left to spin the Pipe model clockwise until the seam is hidden.

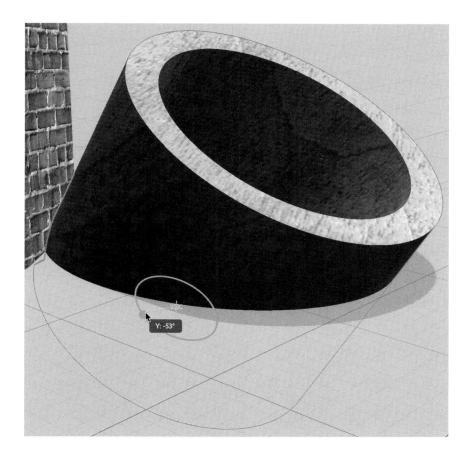

Too much (or too little) surface detail in the material

Materials generated by Adobe Capture contain a "normal map." This is a bitmap file that controls how the surface affects light and shadows. The contrast between light and dark areas in the bitmap affects the visible difference between the "high points" and "low points" on the surface texture. This effect is most noticeable when sunlight hits the surface at certain angles.

In this scene, when sunlight hits the brick material, the white mortar appears to ooze out between the bricks.

1   Hover over the Prism model, and click the right arrow icon  to reveal the material applied to the prism.

2   In the Properties panel, click the image swatch next to Normal. This reveals the bitmap that is the normal map.

Normal

3   Click the pencil icon to edit the image in Photoshop.

4   In Photoshop, choose Image > Adjustments > Brightness/Contrast.

5 Select the Use Legacy option, and then enter a value of **−75** for the Contrast. Adding contrast will make the surface texture more pronounced, and removing contrast will make it less pronounced.

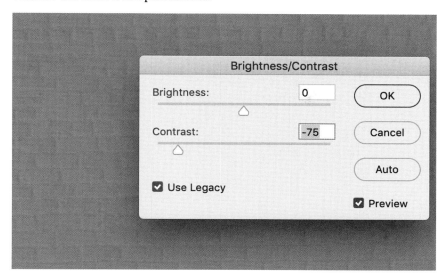

6 Click OK.

7 Choose File > Close, and click Save when prompted.

8 Back in Dimension, click outside the image picker to close it, and you should see that the surface texture is less pronounced.

9 In the Properties panel, click again on the image swatch next to Normal.

10 Click the trash can icon  to remove the Normal bitmap.

11 Now the brick and mortar texture should appear completely flat on the prism model.

Material too flat or too shiny

When you create a material with Adobe Capture, you have some control over how metallic the material is. At first glance, it might appear that you can't edit how metallic a material from Capture is after you've applied it to a model. But if you know a little trick, you can.

1   Hover over the Pipe model, and click the right arrow icon ⟩ to reveal the material applied to the pipe.

In the Properties panel, you'll see that the sliders for Roughness and Metallic are grayed out, which indicates that you can't change them. But here's the trick.

2   Click the properties swatch next to Roughness.

3   Click the trash icon 🗑 to remove the bitmap that came from Capture. Now you can adjust the Roughness slider.

4   Click the properties swatch next to Metallic.

5   Click the trash icon to remove the bitmap that came from Capture. Now you can adjust the Metallic slider.

6 Now you have full control over how smooth and shiny the surface of the model is. Enter **53%** for the Roughness, and **0%** for Metallic.

Review questions

1 When editing a material in Adobe Capture, what does the Metallic slider do?

2 In addition to creating materials from your mobile device camera, what other sources can you use to create materials with Capture?

3 What should you do if a material created with Capture isn't the right size when applied to a model?

4 Why might you see a "seam" displayed on a model after a material has been applied?

Review answers

1 Adjusting the Metallic value controls the degree of metallic luster (shininess) on the surface of the material.

2 You can create a material with Capture from any image that has been saved to your device's camera roll, Creative Cloud storage, Dropbox, or Google Drive. Capture can also access images in Adobe Lightroom and Adobe Stock.

3 To change the size and position of a material that is applied to a model, adjust the Offset, Rotation, or Repeat values in the Properties panel as desired.

4 A seam in the material may be visible if the bitmap image used to create the material isn't large enough to cover the entire model surface. To fix this, you can use the Offset, Rotation, or Repeat values in the Properties panel, or reposition the object to hide the seam.

8 SELECTING OBJECTS AND SURFACES

Lesson overview

In this lesson, you'll explore how to select objects and surfaces on the canvas and learn the following:

- Two different ways to use the Select tool to select objects on the canvas.

- How to use tool options to modify the behavior of the Select tool.

- How to restrict your selection to only certain models within a model group.

- How to quickly align and distribute multiple selected models.

- How to precisely select specific surfaces of a model.

- How to break apart a single model into multiple submodels.

This lesson will take about 45 minutes to complete. To get the lesson files used in this chapter, download them from the web page for this book at www.adobepress.com/DimensionCIB2020. For more information, see "Accessing the lesson files and Web Edition" in the Getting Started section at the beginning of this book.

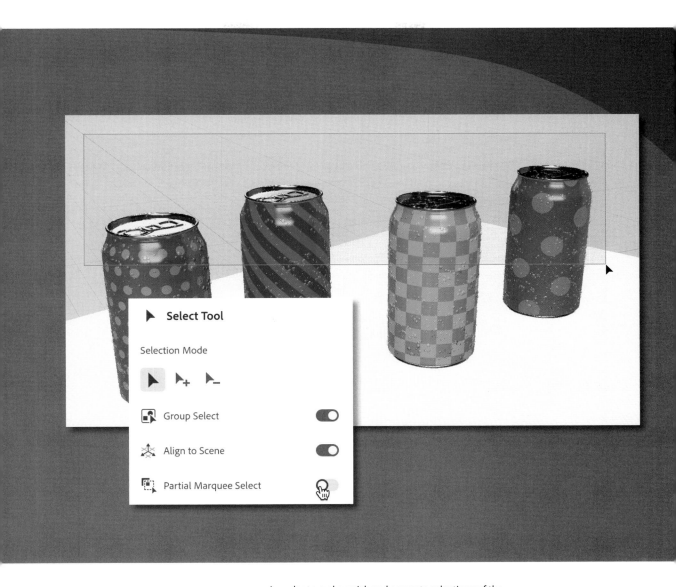

In order to make quick and accurate selections of the
models in your scene, it is important to understand
the options provided by the Select tool.

Using the Selection tools to select objects

In previous lessons, you have usually selected models by clicking the name of the model or the model group in the Scene panel. I'm in the habit of making most of my selections this way, as it has three distinct advantages. First, it is very precise. When you use this selection method, you'll end up selecting the model or models you want, and nothing extra. Second, it makes you focus on the Scene panel as you work, which has the added benefit of making you aware of how your models are grouped, which models are locked, and which are hidden. It is a best practice to frequently refer to the Scene panel as you work on a complex project. Third, you're able to select models and groups via the Scene panel regardless of which tool you have selected at the moment. You can select an object while the Orbit tool is selected, for example.

But sometimes it's quicker or more convenient to select models and groups directly on the canvas. You use the Select tool to do this, of course. But you should be aware of the subtleties of how this works.

Selecting multiple objects by clicking

Let's look closely at the various options for selecting objects on the canvas with the Select tool.

1 Choose File > Open.

2 Select the file named Lesson_08_begin.dn, which is in the Lessons > Lesson08 folder that you copied onto your hard disk, and then click Open.

In the Scene panel you'll see that this scene consists of five model groups (four cans and a table) as well as models of a banana and a floor.

3 So that you don't accidentally select the table in the next few steps, hover over the Table group in the Scene panel, and click the light gray lock icon 🔒 to lock the group.

4 To zoom in on the cans, click the Camera Bookmarks icon ⭐ and click the "Four cans" bookmark.

5 Select the Select tool (keyboard shortcut: V).

6 Click the red can to select it. You can tell that it is selected because the Select widget appears on the can, and the "Red can" model group is highlighted in the Scene panel.

7 Right-click the Select tool in the Tools panel, and click the Add To Selection icon ▶+ under Selection Mode.

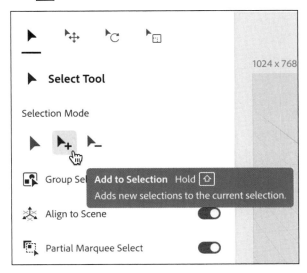

8 Click away from the tool options box to dismiss it.

9 Click the blue can, and you'll see that it is added to the selection. The select widget moves to a common center between the two models, and both models become highlighted in the Scene panel.

10 Click the green can and then the purple can so that all the cans are selected.

11 Right-click the Select tool in the Tools panel, and click the Subtract From Selection icon ![icon].

12 Click away from the tool options box to dismiss it.

13 Click the green can to deselect it. You should now have three cans selected, and you can verify this in the Scene panel.

> **Tip:** Instead of right-clicking the Select tool and choosing the Add To Selection or Subtract From Selection icons, it is much more convenient to add to a selection by holding down the Shift key and clicking a model that isn't yet selected, and to subtract from a selection by holding down the Shift key and clicking a model that is selected.

14 Drag the blue arrow to the left a bit to move all three selected cans. Note that there is no need to group the cans just to move, rotate, or scale them. As long as all three are selected, they can all be transformed at once.

Selecting multiple objects with marquee select

The Add To Selection option is good if you need to surgically select several objects in a crowded scene and need to "skip over" some of the objects while selecting others. But if all your objects are positioned close to each other without other objects in the way, marquee selection is very useful.

1 Choose Edit > Deselect All to deselect the cans.

2   Right-click the Select tool in the Tools panel, and click the New Selection icon  under Selection Mode.

This returns the Select tool behavior to "normal" so that it will not add to or subtract from the selection. After using the Add To Selection or Subtract From Selection buttons, it is easy to forget that they are chosen, causing the selection tools not to function as you are expecting!

3   Click away from the tool options box to dismiss it.

4   Position the mouse somewhere above and to the left of the four cans, and drag a rectangle down and to the right so that the rectangle touches the tops of the cans but nothing else.

Anything that is touched by this selection rectangle, or "band select," is selected. You should see in the Scene panel that all four cans are selected. Note that a can didn't have to be entirely inside the band to be selected. The band needs to touch only part of a model or model group to select the entire model or model group.

● **Note:** The options for the various tools in the Tools panel are "sticky" for the current work session. In other words, if you double-click the Select tool and change the Selection Mode to Add To Selection, that mode will be in effect for the current file, as well as for any other files you work on until you quit Dimension. When you quit, all the tool options are set back to their defaults.

5   Choose Edit > Deselect All to deselect the cans.

6   To change your view of the scene, click the Camera Bookmarks icon and click Banana.

7   Right-click the Select tool in the Tools panel, and click Partial Marquee Select to turn this option off.

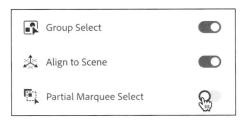

With the Partial Marquee Select option turned off, a model must be entirely surrounded by the selection rectangle to get selected.

Note: There's a good visual cue to help you determine if the Partial Marquee Select option is on or off. When Partial Marquee Select is on, the selection rectangle displays light blue shading. When Partial Marquee Select is off, the selection rectangle is not shaded.

8 Click away from the tool options box to dismiss it.

9 Drag a selection rectangle that touches only part of the banana.

The banana is not selected, because the entire model isn't contained within the selection rectangle.

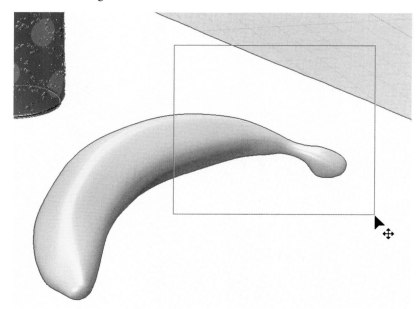

▶ **Tip:** Holding down the Option key (macOS) or Alt key (Windows) while you drag with the Select tool will toggle you to the opposite marquee select behavior. In other words, if you have Partial Marquee Select turned on, holding down Option/Alt will turn it off.

10 Drag a selection rectangle that entirely encloses the banana. It makes no difference if the rectangle touches a part of one of the cans, but the entire banana must be contained in the band.

Now the banana is selected.

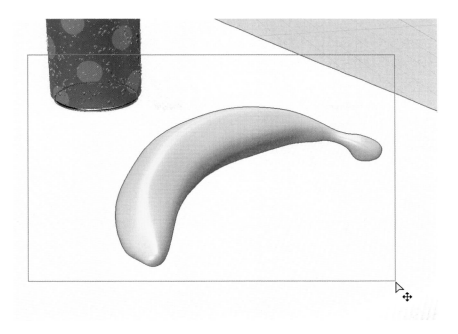

You may notice that the arrows on the move widget aren't aligned with the x-, y-, and z-axes in your scene. This is because the banana was rotated after it was brought into the scene.

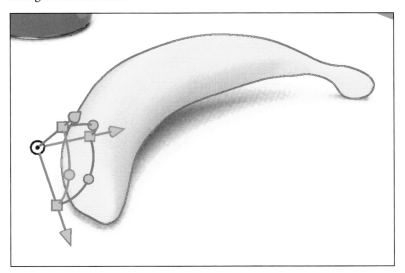

11 To make it easier to move the banana around on the tabletop, choose Object > Align To Scene. Now you should see the arrows on the move widget aligned with the x-, y-, and z-axes.

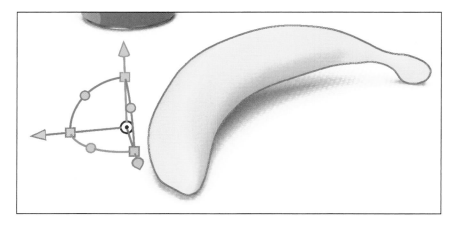

12 Grab the banana (not one of the Select widget arrows) and drag it to move it on the tabletop.

Grabbing an object directly is a really useful way to restrict movement to the x and z axes — in other words, to move it around without raising or lowering it.

You can choose to work with the Partial Marquee Select option on or off. I prefer to leave it on, as this more closely mimics the behavior of the Selection tool in Illustrator and InDesign. However, if you choose to work with the option turned off, you should be aware of how it interacts with a feature called Group Select.

13 With the Partial Marquee Select option still turned off, drag a band select that touches just the middle of one of the cans. When you release the mouse, the can will not be selected. This makes sense, because the entire model wasn't inside your selection rectangle and Partial Marquee Select is turned off.

14 Drag another selection rectangle, but this time enclose the top of one of the cans. When you release the mouse button, you might be surprised to see that the can is selected. But why? The entire can wasn't enclosed in the selection marquee, so why was it selected?

If you look closely at the Scene panel, you'll see that each can is a model group made of three models: a Pull Ring model, a Liquid model, and a Can model. When you dragged your selection marquee around the top of the can, *the Pull Ring model was entirely enclosed in the selection rectangle,* so that model was selected. And then, by extension, the entire model group was selected since the Group Select option was also turned on in the Select tool options. When this option is on, selecting a model in a group selects the entire group. You will learn more about the Group Select option in the following section.

📁 Purple can
    ⬡ Pull Ring
    ⬡ Liquid
    ⬡ Can

Selecting one model in a group

Normally, when you click a model on the canvas, if that model is part of a model group, the entire model group is selected. This is because the Group Select option for the selection tools is turned on by default. Let's see what happens when you turn this option off.

1   To change your view of the scene, choose Camera > Switch To Home View.

2   With the Select tool, click the tablecloth on the canvas. Look in the Scene panel, and you'll see that the entire Table group is selected.

3   To unlock the Table group, choose Object > Lock/Unlock.

4   Choose Edit > Deselect All to deselect the model group.

5   Right-click the Select tool in the Tools panel, and turn off the Group Select option.

6   Click away from the tool options box to dismiss it.

7   Click the tablecloth on the canvas.

Now only the Tablecloth model is selected, as you can see in the Scene panel.

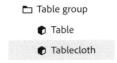

8   Choose Edit > Deselect All to deselect the model.

9   Right-click the Select tool in the Tools panel, and turn the Group Select option back on.

10 Click away from the tool options box to dismiss it.

11 Hold down the Command key (macOS) or Ctrl key (Windows) and click the tablecloth on the canvas. Only the Tablecloth model is selected, not the Table group. Holding down the Command/Ctrl key and clicking a model restricts the selection to a single model within a group, the same as turning off the Group Select option.

▶ **Tip:** When you have a model in a group selected, pressing the Esc key selects the parent group that the model is in.

Recommended Select tool settings for Illustrator and InDesign users

Use these settings if you're an expert Illustrator or InDesign user, and you want the Select tool in Dimension to behave as much as possible like the Selection tool in Illustrator and InDesign.

- Selection Mode: New Selection.

  Press the Shift key while clicking on an object to add that object to the current selection. Press the Option key (macOS) or Alt key (Windows) while clicking on a selected object to remove the object from the selection.

- Partial Marquee Select: On.

  Press the Option key (macOS) or Alt key (Windows) while you drag with the Select tool to temporarily turn Partial Marquee Select off.

- Group Select: Off.

  Command-click (macOS) or Ctrl-click (Windows) on an object in a group to select just that object, not the entire group.

Aligning models

You may want to precisely align models to each other, or evenly distribute the spacing between models. Dimension has an alignment widget that is very helpful for this common task.

1 Select all four cans again, using whatever method you wish (shift-clicking with the Select tool on the models on the canvas or in the Scene panel, or marquee selection).

2 If you are no longer zoomed in on the cans, click the Camera Bookmarks icon 📷 and click the "Four cans" bookmark.

▶ Tip: "A" is the keyboard shortcut for Align And Distribute.

3 Click the Align And Distribute icon  in the Actions panel. You should see the Align And Distribute widget appear surrounding the four cans.

4 Hover over the middle magenta teardrop handle. You'll see a blue plane highlight near the cans. This highlight indicates the plane to which the cans will align when you click this icon.

5 Click the middle magenta teardrop handle to align the center of each can to the same plane.

6   Single-click the blue bar to distribute the four cans evenly between the leftmost and rightmost can.

7   Double-click the blue bar to apply a spacing of 0 to each can.

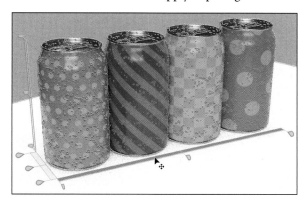

8   Drag any of the blue teardrop handles to the right or left until the spacing is the way you want it.

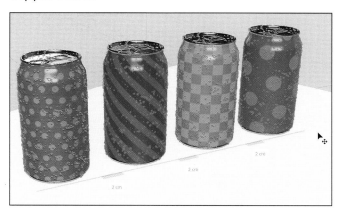

Using the Magic Wand tool to select surfaces

While the Select tool is used to select models and model groups, the Magic Wand tool is used to select individual surfaces on a model. As you'll see, it works a lot like the Magic Wand tool in Adobe Photoshop.

1 Choose Camera > Switch To Home View so that you can see the entire table.

2 In the Scene panel, click the closed model group icon 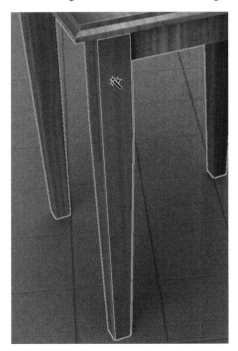 next to the Table group to open the group.

3 Hover over the Tablecloth model, and click the eye icon to hide the tablecloth.

4 Double-click the Magic Wand tool and change the Selection Size to Tiny.

5 Click away from the tool options box to dismiss it.

6 Click somewhere on the table leg closest to the camera.

You'll see that part of the surface of the leg is selected. The surface that is selected is indicated by the blue tinted fill, not the blue outline. Depending on where you clicked, a different amount may be selected than pictured here, and that's okay. The Magic Wand tool tries to determine different parts of a model surface based on edges and similarity of tone. You want the entire leg selected, but the Magic Wand didn't select enough.

7 Right-click the Magic Wand tool in the Tools panel.

8 Drag the Selection Size slider all the way to the right, to Large.

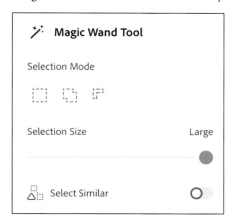

9 Click away from the tool options box to dismiss it.

10 Click again on the leg, and this time the entire leg should be selected.

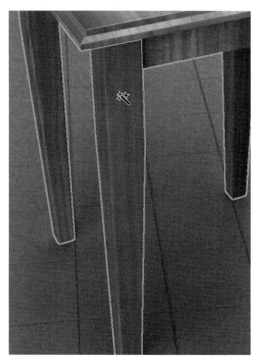

The attributes of a particular model and what you are trying to select will determine what works best for the Selection Size slider. I usually leave this set to Tiny, and then use the following technique to increase the size of the selection.

11 Right-click the Magic Wand tool in the Tools panel again.

12 Drag the Selection Size slider all the way back to the left, to the Tiny setting.

13 Click away from the tool options box to dismiss it.

14 Click the top surface of the tabletop with the Magic Wand tool. With the Selection Size slider set to Tiny, only the top part of the tabletop is selected, not the edges.

15 Hold down the Shift key, and click one of the edge surfaces of the tabletop. This adds that area to the selection. If any other portions of the tabletop need to be added to the selection, Shift-click them. If any areas of the table become selected that shouldn't be selected, hold down the Option key (macOS) or Alt key (Windows) to remove the area from the selection.

An alternative to holding down the Shift key or Option/Alt key to add to or take away from a selection is to right-click the Magic Wand tool, click either the Add To Selection or Subtract From Selection button, and then click the model. But it is much easier to Shift-click an unselected surface to add it to the selection or to Option/Alt-click a selected surface to remove it from the selection.

Changing the material applied to a surface

Now that the tabletop surface is selected separately from the rest of the model, you can change the material applied to it.

1. In the Content panel, select the Valencia Marble SBSAR material (in the starter assets) to change the top of the table from wood to marble.

2. Select the Orbit tool (keyboard shortcut: 1).

3. Drag up and to the right to rotate the camera view so you can see a little more of the left side of the table. Something like this.

4. The vertical wood grain on the horizontal "skirt" pieces under the tabletop looks a bit strange. You'll fix this next. With the Magic Wand tool, click the wooden skirt piece under the left side of the tabletop.

5 Hold down the Shift key and click the second skirt piece.

6 Choose Edit > Cut. This actually cuts, or deletes, the skirt pieces from the table model. However, you won't see them disappear, since you only had the front face of each piece selected. This will meet our needs for this lesson. If you really needed to delete the entire skirt board, you would need to zoom in and reposition the camera so that you could select all the different faces of the board with the Magic Wand tool.

7 Choose Edit > Paste. This will paste the skirt piece back in place. It will look like nothing has changed. But if you look in the Scene panel, you'll see that there is a new model named "Side Table" at the bottom of the panel. This is the model that you just separated from the rest of the model by cutting and pasting.

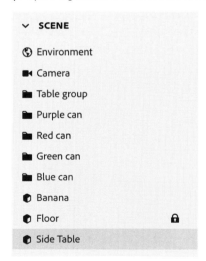

8 Double-click the new Side Table model in the Scene panel to rename it, type **Skirt Pieces**, and press Return/Enter.

9 To keep things organized, drag the Skirt Pieces model up onto the Table group to add it to the group.

10 The reason for doing all this is so that the material on the skirt pieces can be manipulated separately from the material applied to the rest of the table. If it is closed, click the closed model group icon ◼ next to the Table group to open the group.

11 Hover over the Skirt Pieces model, and click the right arrow icon ⟩ to reveal the model materials.

12 In the Properties panel, under Offset, change the rotation angle to **−90°** and press Enter/Return.

Now the grain on the table skirt pieces should run in the right direction.

13 In the Properties panel, under Repeat, change the X and Y values to **2.2** and press Enter/Return. This will make the grain look more realistic.

You may wonder why you had to cut and paste the skirt pieces to create separate objects, but you didn't need to cut and paste the tabletop. You can always apply a new material to any selected surface of a model (like you did to the tabletop), without affecting the rest of the model surfaces. While you had the table top selected, you could have cut and pasted it, just for convenience for working with the model later. But it wasn't required.

With the skirt pieces, however, if you had attempted to rotate the material right after you selected them, the Cherry Wood material for the entire table would have rotated. To change material properties of just part of a model, you must separate the model into separate objects via cut and paste.

This ability to "break apart" models into separate pieces, delete pieces, and rearrange pieces is an important capability of Dimension, making your models much more flexible.

Review questions

1. Aside from using the Add To Selection and Remove from Selection buttons in the selection tool options, how can you select multiple models on the canvas?

2. If you want a marquee selection to select only models that are entirely enclosed in the marquee, should the Partial Marquee Select option be turned on or off?

3. To select only a single model (not the entire group) when the Group Select option is on, what key should you hold down while clicking a model within a group?

4. What should you do if the Select tool widget displayed on a model on the canvas isn't aligned with the x-, y-, and z-axes of your scene, making it difficult to transform your model?

5. How do you break a portion of a model away from the main model into a separate "sub" model?

Review answers

1. Press the Shift key while clicking an additional model to add that model to an existing selection. Or press the Shift key while clicking a selected model to remove that model from the selection.

2. Turning the Partial Marquee Select option off in the Select tool options will cause a marquee select to select only models that are entirely enclosed in the marquee selection rectangle.

3. Hold down the Command key (macOS) or Ctrl key (Windows) while clicking a model in a model group to select only the model, not the entire group.

4. When the Select tool widget doesn't display as expected on a model on the canvas, Choose Object > Align To Scene.

5. To break apart a model, select part of the model with the Magic Wand tool, and then choose Edit > Cut and Edit > Paste.

9 APPLYING GRAPHICS TO MODELS

Lesson overview

In this lesson, you'll explore and apply graphics to model surfaces and learn the following:

- What types of graphics can be applied to the surface of a model.
- The differences between graphics and materials.
- How to edit a graphic after it has been applied.
- How to apply multiple graphics to a model surface.
- How to restrict the application of graphics to specific model surfaces.

This lesson will take about 45 minutes to complete. To get the lesson files used in this chapter, download them from the web page for this book at www.adobepress.com/DimensionCIB2020. For more information, see "Accessing the lesson files and Web Edition" in the Getting Started section at the beginning of this book.

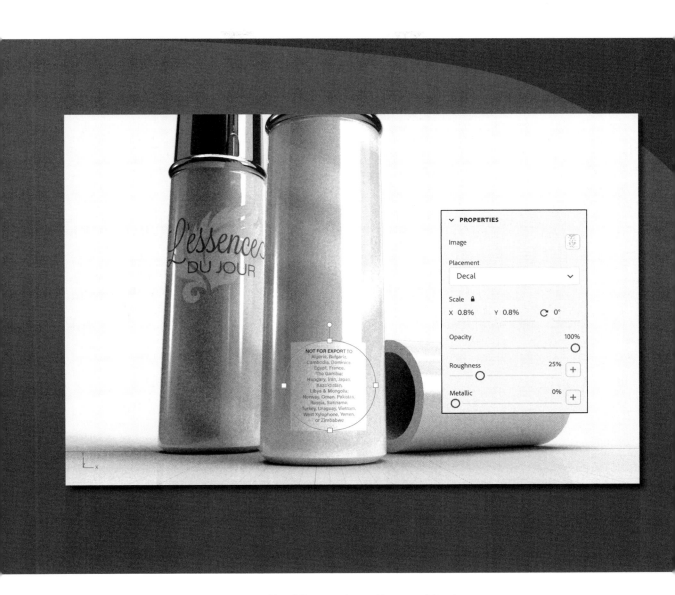

The ability to apply graphics to model surfaces opens
all kinds of possibilities for adding labels and other
artwork to your models.

Beginning a new project and importing a model

A common task in package design is mocking up a specific type of package with the artwork that is going to be printed on, or affixed to, the package. Since you can import and apply graphics to the surfaces of models, Dimension is useful for this workflow. In this lesson, you will apply background artwork and labels to a perfume bottle.

1   In Adobe Dimension, choose File > New With Settings. This command lets you specify the canvas size and other attributes as you create a new file.

2   In the New Document dialog, under Canvas Size, change the width to **3000 px** and the height to **2000 px**. Increasing the pixel dimensions will make your label artwork look much better.

3   Deselect the Set As Default option, and click Create.

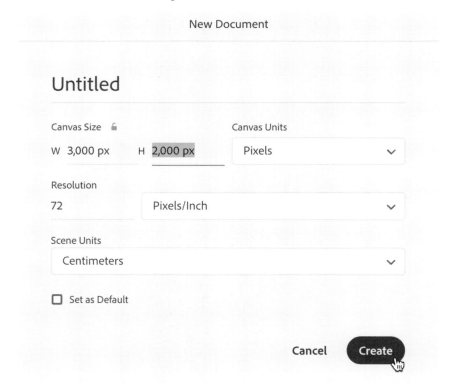

4   Click the Add And Import Content icon ⊕ at the top of the Tools panel.

5   Select Adobe Stock.

6   Select Browse All Adobe Stock 3D.

Your default browser will launch, and you'll be brought to a page on stock.adobe.com.

7 In your browser on the Adobe Stock page, type **208142389** into the search field and press Return/Enter.

This is the ID number of a perfume bottle model used in this lesson. This model is free.

8 Click the License For Free button. The asset will be licensed, and downloaded to your browser's download location.

9 In Dimension, choose File > Import > 3D Model.

10 Navigate to your browser's default download location, open the folder named AdobeStock_208142389, select the file named portable_perfume_spray_1460.obj, and click Open. The model will be placed in the center of the scene, positioned on the ground plane.

11 Choose Camera > Frame All to position the camera on the model.

Organizing the model components

When you place a model in a scene, the first thing you should do is examine the model in the Scene panel to see how it's put together. Is it a single model, or a group of models? Are the models labeled in a way that makes sense to you? Taking a few moments to become familiar with the model will pay off as you incorporate it into your scene.

▶ **Tip:** You can also hide or show a model by selecting the model and pressing the Command+; (macOS) or Ctrl+; (Windows) keyboard shortcut.

1   In the Scene panel, you'll see that the model is a group named portable_perfume_spray_1460. Double-click the name of the model group and change the name to **Bottle**.

2   Click the closed model group icon ▇ to open the group.

3   Hover over each of the models in the group, and click the eye icon 👁 twice to hide and show the model to help you identify which model is which.

4   Change the name of the middle model in the group to **Nozzle**. Change the name of the bottom model in the group to **Spray top**.

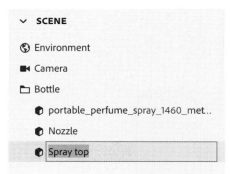

Note that the top model in the Scene panel contains both the body of the perfume bottle and the bottle cap. It would be useful to work with these separately, so you'll break them apart.

5   Right-click or double-click the Magic Wand tool in the Tools panel.

6   Set the Selection Size to Large.

7   Click away from the tool option panel to dismiss it.

8 Click once on the bottle cap on the canvas to select it.

9 Choose Edit > Cut. The bottle cap should disappear.

10 Choose Edit > Paste. The bottle cap will be pasted in the same location, but now it is a separate model, as you can see in the Scene panel.

11 Double-click the new model in the Scene panel, and type **Bottle cap** for the model name.

12 Double-click the model named portable_perfume_spray_1460_metal_black and rename it **Body**.

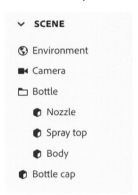

13 Select the Select tool (keyboard shortcut: V).

14 Select the Bottle cap model.

15 Hold down the Shift key, and drag the blue circle on the Select tool widget clockwise to rotate the bottle cap model until it is lying on its side. Holding down the Shift key constrains rotation to 15° increments, making it easy to rotate the model exactly −90°.

16 Drag the green circle on the Select tool widget counter-clockwise to rotate the bottle cap 30° or so.

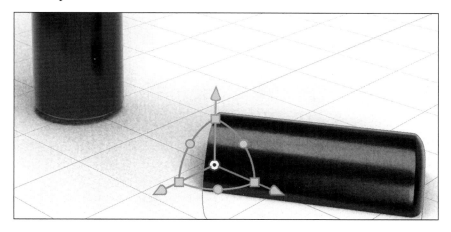

17 Choose Object > Move To Ground to position the bottle cap on the ground plane.

18 Select the Bottle group, and Choose Object > Move To Ground to position the bottle on the ground plane.

19 Select the Orbit tool (keyboard shortcut: 1).

20 Drag to the right to rotate the view so you are looking straight at the front of the spray bottle.

21 Click the Camera Bookmarks icon ⊞ at the top of the screen.

22 Click the plus icon $\boxed{+}$ to create a new bookmark.

23 To rename the bookmark, type **Front view** and press Return/Enter. This will allow you to easily return to this view at any time.

24 Choose File > Save to save the file with a name and location that will allow you to find it later.

Applying a background graphic

In previous lessons you learned how to apply materials to the surface of a model to change its look. Materials can contain all kinds of properties, such as glow, roughness, metallic luster, and translucence, as well as color and pattern. A graphic is another way to apply color and pattern to a model surface, and this color and pattern works in concert with the model's surface material.

Files in AI (Adobe Illustrator), PSD (Adobe Photoshop), JPEG, PNG, SVG, or TIFF format can be placed as graphics on the surface of a model.

1 In the Scene panel, select the Body model.

2 In the Actions panel, click the Place Graphic On Model icon $\boxed{\text{C}}$.

Tip: Before placing a graphic on a model, always position the camera so that it is pointed straight at the surface on which you want to position the graphic. The camera view affects where the graphic "lands" when it is placed on the model.

3 Select the file named Background_label.psd, which is in the Lessons > Lesson09 folder that you copied onto your hard disk, and then click Open.

The label is placed on the body of the spray can, visible to your current view at the size of your model. The label is surrounded by a round selection widget that makes it easy to resize, rotate, or move the label on the model. If you don't see the selection widget as pictured here, select the Select tool in the Tools panel (keyboard shortcut: V).

4 Graphics arrive by default applied as a "decal" to models. But you can also fill the surface of a model with a graphic. In the Properties panel, choose Fill from the Placement menu.

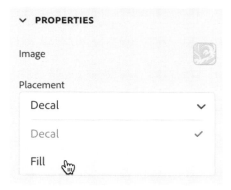

This causes the graphic to scale proportionally until it fills the entire model surface.

5 You can also choose to tile a smaller graphic across a model surface. To see how this works, enter **10** for the X and Y Repeat values in the Properties panel.

You'll see the rectangular graphic repeat in a tile pattern across the surface of the model.

6 Under Placement in the Properties panel, change Repeat to Mirror.

This will cause the tiles to mirror both horizontally and vertically across the model surface.

Repeat fill   Mirror fill

7 Change the X and Y values for repeat back to **1** so that one large instance of the graphic fills the model surface.

8   Examine the Scene panel. Note that the Body model now contains both a material (the original material, named portable_perfume_spray_1460_metal_black_MatSG_Mat) and the graphic that you just placed.

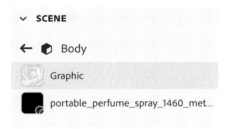

Applying additional graphics

A single model surface can contain as many graphics as you wish. Next, you'll add two more labels to the body of the perfume bottle.

1   In the Actions panel, click the Place Graphic On Model icon ⌞▣⌟.

2   Select the file named Lessence_du_jour_label.ai and then click Open.

3   Hold down the Shift key, and drag one of the four selection handles on the widget inward to make the label smaller. Holding down the Shift key constrains the scaling to be proportional.

4   Drag anywhere inside the selection circle to move the label around on the surface of the model until it is positioned as desired.

Note that the Scene panel now lists two graphics, as well as the original material applied to the perfume bottle body.

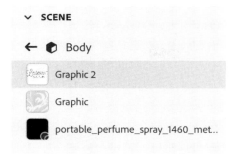

5 Double-click Graphic 2 and change the name to **Lessence label graphic**.

6 Double-click Graphic and change the name to **Background graphic**.

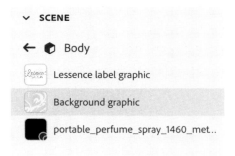

▶ **Tip:** Always take a moment to name models, groups, materials, and graphics in the Scene panel. This added clarity will pay off later on when you need to perform further editing in the file.

7 Select the Orbit tool in the Tools panel (keyboard shortcut: 1).

8 Drag from left to right across the screen until you can see the back side of the spray can.

9 In the Actions panel, click the Place Graphic On Model icon 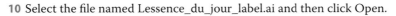.

10 Select the file named Lessence_du_jour_label.ai and then click Open.

Since this is the same file you placed on the front of the can, you get another copy of the L'essence du Jour label on the back of the can. But this is an Illustrator file that contains multiple artboards, and you can choose a different artboard after the graphic is placed.

11 In the Properties panel, click the image swatch next to the word "Image."

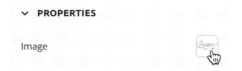

12 Choose Artboard 2 from the list of artboards.

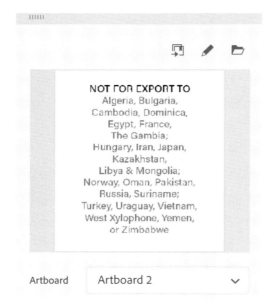

13 Use the Select tool to scale and position the label as desired.

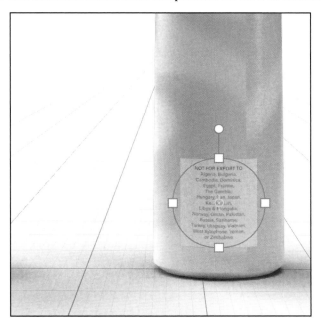

Note that there are now three graphics listed in the Scene panel. You can change the stacking order of these graphics.

14 Drag Graphic 3 below Background graphic in the list, and you'll see that Background graphic covers up Graphic 3 on the model.

▶ **Tip:** You can also drag and drop graphic files from the Macintosh Finder or Windows File Explorer onto a model to place the graphic on the model surface. Or you can copy and paste a graphic from Photoshop or Illustrator onto a selected model in Dimension.

15 Drag Graphic 3 back up to the top of the list so that it is visible again.

Modifying graphic properties

Each graphic can have its own properties for opacity, roughness, and metallic luster.

1 Click the Camera Bookmarks icon  at the top of the screen.

2 Select Front View to return to viewing the front of the spray can.

3 Choose Background graphic in the Scene panel.

4 In the Properties panel, change the Roughness value to **10%** and the Metallic value to **10%**. This affects only the background graphic.

5 In the Scene panel, select the Lessence label graphic.

6 In the Properties panel, enter **90%** for the Roughness value to give the label a flatter finish.

Editing a label in Illustrator

After you've placed a graphic on a model, you can do round-trip editing of the file in Illustrator or Photoshop. If you've placed an AI or SVG graphic on a model, it will open in Illustrator for editing. If you've placed a JPEG, PNG, PSD, or TIFF image, it will open in Photoshop. After you edit the graphic, it will automatically update on the model.

1 In the Scene panel, select the Lessence label graphic.

2 In the Properties panel, click the image swatch next to the word "Image."

3 In the box that appears, double-click the image or click the pencil icon ✏️ to edit the graphic in Illustrator.

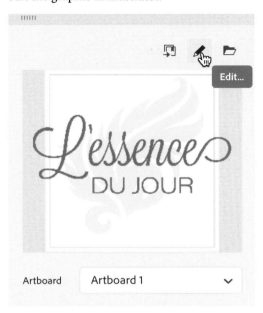

4 In Illustrator, delete the white box that is behind the image, or make any other edit to the image that you wish.

5 In Illustrator, choose File > Close, and, when prompted, save the file.

In Dimension, you should see the label update to reflect the changes you made in Illustrator.

Finishing the scene

Now you'll add a few final touches to the scene, including colors and lighting.

1 Select the Select tool in the Tools panel (keyboard shortcut: V).

2 Click somewhere on the background area around the model to select the environment.

3 In the Properties panel, click the color swatch next to the word "Background."

4 Click the Color Sampler icon ⟨icon⟩ in the lower-right corner of the color picker.

5 Click a pink area of the L'essence Du Jour label to sample the pink color and apply it to the scene background.

6 Double-click the Bottle cap model on the canvas to display the Bottle cap materials.

7 Click the color swatch next to Base Color in the Properties panel.

8 Click the Color tab.

9 Click the Color Sampler icon in the lower-right corner of the color picker.

10 Click a blue area of the Body model to sample the color and apply it to the bottle cap.

11 In the Starter Assets panel, click the lights icon to display only lights in the panel.

12 Select 3-Point Light to apply it to the scene.

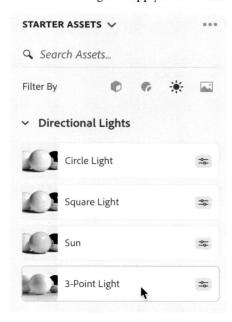

13 Select Environment Light in the Scene panel.

14 Click the Delete icon 🗑 in the Actions panel.

15 Select Environment in the Scene panel.

16 In the Properties panel, change the Reflection Opacity for the Ground Plane to **10%**.

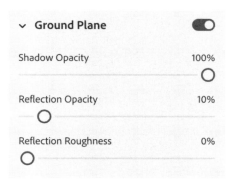

17 Use the Select tool to move the Bottle cap closer to the perfume bottle.

18 Use the camera tools to adjust the camera angle as desired.

Using advanced techniques

In this lesson you'll learn some advanced techniques for working with placed graphics. You'll learn how to stack semi-transparent graphics, how to control where on a model a graphic is initially applied, and how to restrict the application of a graphic image to only certain surfaces on a model.

Begin a new project and import a model

You'll begin by creating a new file and placing a free model of a serving plate from Adobe Stock in the scene.

1 In Adobe Dimension, choose File > New With Settings.

2 In the New Document dialog, under Canvas Size, change the width to **3000 px** and the height to **2000 px**.

3 Deselect the Set As Default option, and click Create.

4   Click the Add And Import Content icon  at the top of the Tools panel.

5   Select Adobe Stock.

6   Select Browse All Adobe Stock 3D.

7   In your browser on the Adobe Stock page, type **178262437** into the search field and press Return/Enter.

    This is the ID number of a serving plate model used in this lesson. This model is free.

8   Click the License For Free button. The asset will be licensed, and downloaded to your browser's download location.

9   In Dimension, choose File > Import > 3D Model.

10 Navigate to your browser's default download location, open the folder named AdobeStock_178262437, select the file named e_serving_plate_075.obj, and click Open. The model will be placed in the center of the scene, positioned on the ground plane.

11 Choose Camera > Frame Selection to fit the plate model on the screen.

Placing overlapping graphics on the model

Any surface of a model can have multiple graphics applied to it. Transparency in the graphics is supported, so if a graphic is semi-transparent, any graphics or materials underneath will partially show through.

1   Select the Orbit tool (keyboard shortcut: 1) and use it to position your view of the scene so that you are looking directly down on the top of the plate. You may need to choose Camera > Frame Selection again after doing this so you can see the entire plate on the canvas.

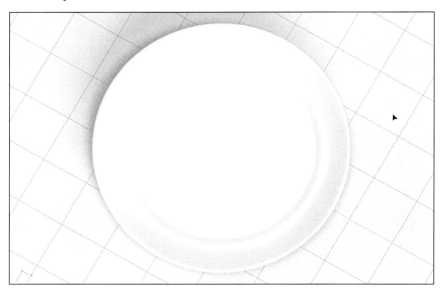

When you place a graphic on a model, Dimension will attempt to center the graphic on the surface of the model that is facing the camera. So it usually works best if you point the camera squarely at the location on the model where you want to place the graphic. That way, less adjustment of the graphic will be required after it is placed.

2   Select the Select tool (keyboard shortcut: V) and double-click the plate model on the canvas. This will select the material applied to the surface of the serving plate model.

3   Click the Place Graphic On Model icon ▣ in the Actions panel.

4   Select the Blue_watercolors.png file and then click Open.

This PNG file was created in Photoshop and consists of a transparent background with several semi-transparent brush strokes created with a watercolor brush.

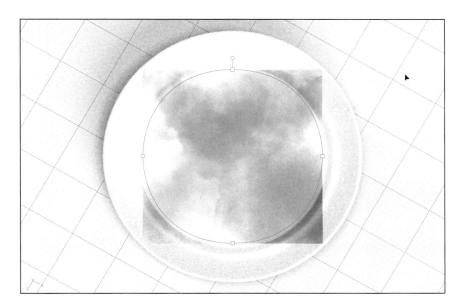

5　Grab one of the selection handles on the placed graphic, hold down the Shift key, and drag the handle out to make the graphic large enough to cover the top surface of the plate.

Holding down the Shift key causes the graphic image to scale proportionally.

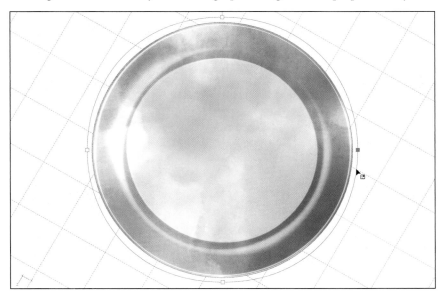

6　Click the Place Graphic On Model icon ▣ in the Actions panel.

7　Again, select the Blue_watercolors.png file and then click Open.

8 Grab one of the selection handles on the placed graphic, hold down the Shift key, and drag the handle out to make the graphic large enough to cover the top surface of the plate.

Now you have two copies of the watercolor graphic placed on top of each other. Because the graphic is semi-transparent, they create a rich layered look. You can see both copies in the Scene panel.

Now you'll rotate one of the copies so that the overlapping semi-transparent strokes create an interesting texture.

9 Grab the rotation handle at the top of the placed graphic, and pull to rotate the graphic so that the two graphics aren't lined up exactly on top of each other.

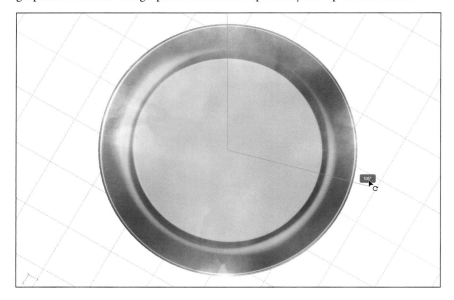

10 Click the Place Graphic On Model icon ⬚ in the Actions panel.

11 Select the Floral_border.ai file, and then click Open.

12 Size and position the floral border on the plate as desired.

13 In the Properties panel, enter **40%** for the Opacity to make the floral border semi-transparent.

14 In the Scene panel, you should see all three graphics stacked up above the e_serving_plate_075_Mat material. Select this material.

15 In the Properties panel, click the color swatch next to the words Base Color, and change the color to **230** red, **255** green, and **230** blue.

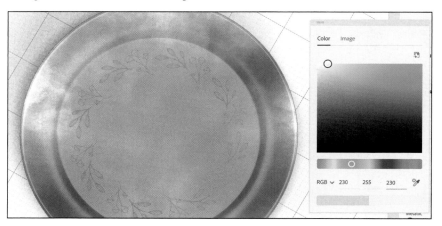

Fixing graphic overlap

When applying graphics to models, its common for the graphic to "overlap" or wrap around to an area or surface of the model where you don't want the graphic to appear. Here's a technique that can help fix the problem.

1 Press Esc to exit the Materials view in the Scene panel and instead display the models. The e_serving_plate_075 model should be selected.

2 In the Properties panel, type **180°** for the X Rotation value. This will flip the plate over.

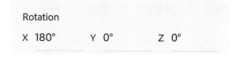

▶ **Tip:** The keyboard shortcut for Move To Ground, Command+period (macOS) or Ctrl+period (Windows) is a good shortcut to learn, as you'll use this command frequently.

3 Choose Object > Move To Ground.

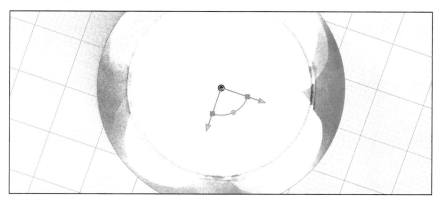

You can see that the graphics you added to the top of the plate wrap around onto the sides of the plate. This is because the entire plate surface is a single model with a single applied material.

Ideally, before you applied the materials to the plate, you would have used the Magic Wand tool, Edit > Cut, and Edit > Paste to break the plate model into three separate models (top, sides, and bottom). That would have prevented the problem. If you break apart the model now, you'll likely need to reposition the graphics on the top surface since the geometry of the model changes when you break it apart. Luckily, there is another technique we can use to restrict the application of the graphic to only the top surface of the plate.

4 Right-click or double-click the Magic Wand tool in the Tools panel.

5 Set the Selection Size to Tiny.

6 Click away from the tool option panel to dismiss it.

7 Click once on the side area of the plate to select it.

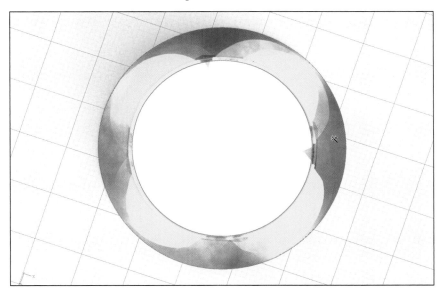

8 Click the Add And Import Content icon at the top of the Tools panel, and choose Starter Assets.

9 Click the Plastic material in the Content panel to apply it to the selected area of
the plate.

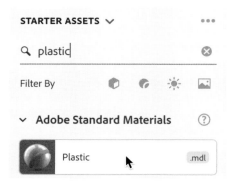

Since a graphic applies only to a single material on a model, the graphics no
longer wrap onto the slides of the plate.

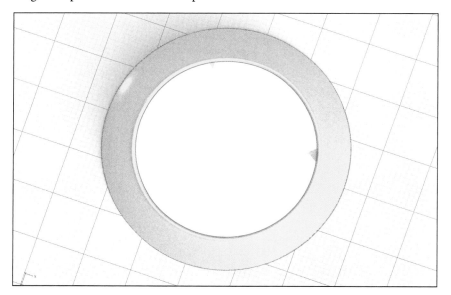

10 With the Magic Wand tool, click the bottom center of the plate to select it.

11 In the Content panel, click the Plastic material to apply it to the bottom area of
the plate.

12 Choose Edit > Deselect All.

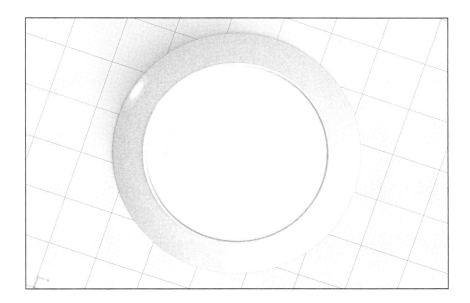

Adjusting material properties

1   With the Select tool, double-click the plate model on the canvas to reveal the materials applied to the plate in the Scene panel. You'll see the three materials (e_serving_plate_075_mat, Plastic, and Plastic 2) applied to the individual surfaces of the plate, each separated by a horizontal line. One or more graphics can be applied to each material on a model independently.

2   Double-click the Plastic 2 material in the Scene panel, type **Bottom material**, and press Return/Enter to rename the material.

3   In the Properties panel, click the color swatch next to Base Color, and change the color to **90** red, **50** green, and **50** blue.

4   In the Properties panel, change the Roughness value to **100%**.

5   Click the Place Graphic On Model icon in the Actions panel.

6   Select the Penguin_pottery_logo.svg file and then click Open.

7   Size and position the logo on the plate as desired.

8   With the logo still selected, change the Roughness value to **100%** in the Properties panel.

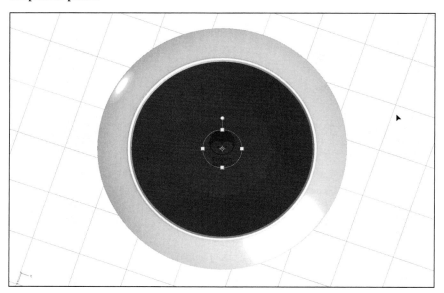

Now, in the Scene panel, you'll see that the Bottom material has the logo graphic (named Graphic 4) applied to it.

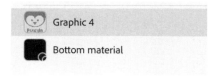

9   Press the Esc key twice to exit the Materials view in the Scene panel and instead display the models. The e_serving_plate_075 model should be selected.

10 In the Properties panel, type **180°** for the X Rotation value. This will flip the plate over.

11 Choose Object > Move To Ground.

12 Select the Orbit tool (keyboard shortcut: 1), and drag up on the canvas so that you can see the side of the plate as well as some of the top.

13 Choose Camera > Frame All.

14 With the Select tool, double-click the plate model on the canvas to reveal the plate materials.

15 Select the Plastic material in the Scene panel.

16 In the Properties panel, click the color swatch next to Base Color.

17 In the color picker, click the Sample Color icon  and click a blue area on the top surface of the plate to sample a blue color and apply it to the sides of the plate.

18 In the Properties panel, increase Roughness to **20%** to make the sides of the plate less shiny.

19 Select the Orbit tool (keyboard shortcut: 1) and examine your finished plate from different angles. You may also want to try duplicating the plate and positioning one of the plates upside-down in the scene as shown below.

Review questions

1   What is the difference between a material and a graphic?

2   What file formats can be used for graphics?

3   When a graphic is placed on the surface of a model, is the image linked to the original graphics file, or does the image become part of the Dimension file?

4   Besides scaling, rotating, or moving a graphic on the model surface, what other properties of a graphic can be changed?

5   If a graphic overlaps an area of the model where you don't want the graphic to appear, what are two techniques you can use to address this?

Review answers

1   Both materials and graphics can be used to apply color and pattern to the surface of a model. But a material can contain specific properties such as glow, roughness, metallic luster, translucence and other properties that add realistic "texture" to the material and affect how light interacts with the material. A graphic is just a flat image that can be wrapped around the surface of the model.

   Multiple materials cannot be applied to a single model surface, but multiple graphics can be applied to each material.

2   Graphic files in AI (Adobe Illustrator), PSD (Adobe Photoshop), JPEG, PNG, SVG, or TIFF file formats can be placed on a model surface.

3   Graphics become part of the Dimension file. They are not linked to the original graphics file.

4   The opacity, roughness, and metallic properties can be adjusted for each graphic applied to a model.

5   If a graphic "bleeds" over a surface of a model where you don't want it to appear, you can often address this by using the Magic Wand tool to select the surface where you don't want the graphic to appear and then either a) cutting and pasting the surface to create a new model from the surface, or b) applying a new material (or another instance of the existing material) to the surface.

10 WORKING WITH BACKGROUNDS

Lesson overview

In this lesson, you'll explore how to add a 2D background image to your scene and learn the following:

- What file formats can be imported.

- What types of images work best as background images.

- How to automatically match your models to a background image so that they look like they belong in the image.

- What to do when the automatic image matching feature can't match the perspective in an image.

 This lesson will take about 45 minutes to complete. To get the lesson files used in this chapter, download them from the web page for this book at www.adobepress.com/DimensionCIB2020. For more information, see "Accessing the lesson files and Web Edition" in the Getting Started section at the beginning of this book.

If you have a background photo with strong, clear perspective lines, Dimension's image-matching features enable you to quickly pose your 3D models in the background.

What you can do with background images

The main purpose of Dimension is to create scenes from one or more 3D models. Every file you create from scratch initially features a plain white background. You can change this background color to whatever you wish, and the color will be applied to the floor (the ground plane) as well as to the rest of the scene background.

However, you can also import a graphic image to be used as a 2D background in your scene. You can use a graphic saved in most of the common image file formats, including AI, JPEG, PNG, PSD, SVG, and TIFF, in the CMYK, RGB, grayscale, or indexed color space.

These background images are static. They remain stationary in the background when you adjust your view of the models in your scene with the camera tools. A common workflow is to compose a 3D scene consisting of some 3D models and then use the camera tools to adjust your perspective and angle of view so that the models appear as if they are part of the background image. As you'll learn in this lesson, Dimension has some powerful features that can help you with this process.

Background image workflows

Sometimes you'll have a particular background image in mind from the start, so you'll import the image into your scene before adding and positioning your models.

Sometimes you'll create a scene with one or more models in Dimension and then decide to add a background image near the end of the project.

And on other occasions you might not be able to locate a suitable background image at all, and you'll decide to construct your own image.

In this lesson, you'll examine each of these workflows.

Starting a project with a background image

You'll begin with a project in which you'll import the background image, specify the camera perspective, and then place the models in the scene.

1 In Adobe Dimension, choose File > New With Settings.

2 In the New Document dialog, under Canvas Size, change the width to **3000 px** and the height to **2000 px**.

3 Deselect the Set As Default option, and click Create.

4 Choose File > Import > Image As Background.

5 Select the Evening_party_tabletop.jpg file, and click Open.

By default, the image arrives centered on the canvas and cropped to fill the canvas. We'll leave the image as it is for this lesson.

6 In the Properties panel, click the Match Image button.

7 Deselect the Resize Canvas To option, select Create Lights and Match Camera Perspective, select Multiple Lights from the Create Lights menu, and then click OK.

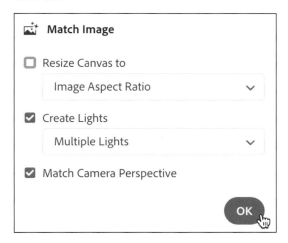

Because of the strong, clear perspective lines created by the boards in the foreground of the photo, Dimension is able to perfectly match the camera perspective to the image. But the grid lines on the ground plane are difficult to see with the photo in the background. Changing the color of the grid lines will help.

8 Select the Select tool (keyboard shortcut: V).

9 Click somewhere in the gray area outside the canvas.

10 Click the color swatch next to Grid in the Properties panel.

11 Change the color to **255** red, **255** green, and **255** blue; then press the Esc key to close the color picker. This will make the grid lines white.

Once you get the camera perspective just right, it is a good practice to save a camera bookmark in case you accidentally change the perspective later while using one of the camera tools.

12 Click the Camera Bookmarks icon  at the top of the screen.

13 Click the plus icon ⊞ to create a new bookmark.

14 To rename the bookmark, type **Ending view** and press Return/Enter.

Examining the auto-generated lights

Dimension uses the background image to automatically extract and build lighting and reflection information for the scene.

1 Click the background image to select the environment.

2 In the Scene panel, select Environment Light.

3 In the Properties panel, click the image swatch to the right of Image.

∨ **PROPERTIES**

Image

This will display the spherical panorama image that Dimension generated automatically from the background image. Dimension uses this bitmap image to create the environment light and reflections.

4 Click away from the image picker to close it.

When you use the Match Image command, Dimension analyzes the image and attempts to choose the right option for the lighting. But you can always override Dimension's choice.

The **Multiple Lights** choice is best for indoor scenes containing windows, lamps, and light fixtures, as well as outdoor nighttime scenes with multiple light sources such as street lamps. The Multiple Lights option will generate one, two, or three directional light sources to match those in the scene.

The **Outdoor Sunlight** option is best for outdoor daylight images, regardless of whether the sun is actually visible in the image. It is usually the best choice for an outdoor scene, even if the scene shows a cloudy day. This choice generates a single Sun light object to match the scene.

The **Abstract** option is good for scenes that don't contain easily identifiable or strong light information. This choice will generate three directional light objects in a traditional three point lighting setup, which you can then modify to suit.

In this case, the Match Image command generated two directional lights using the Multiple Lights option.

5 In the Scene panel, select each of the Directional Lights in turn and view the properties for each in the Properties panel (your automatically-calculated values may differ from the ones shown here).

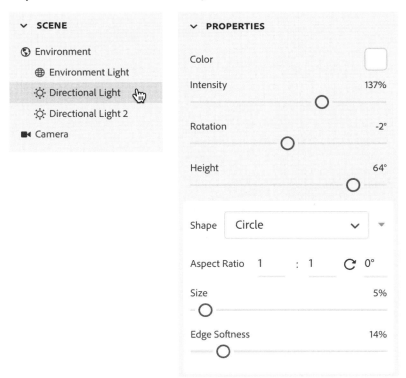

You'll explore the options for environment light, sunlight, and directional lights in another lesson.

Adding models to the scene

Once the background image and perspective are aligned properly, positioning models in the scene is easy.

1 Click the Add And Import Content icon  at the top of the Tools panel.

2 Select Adobe Stock.

3 Select Browse All Adobe Stock 3D.

4 In your browser on the Adobe Stock page, type **182469425** into the search field and press Return/Enter.

5 This is the ID number of a wine glass model. Click the License For Free button. The asset will be licensed, and downloaded to your browser's download location.

6 In your browser on the Adobe Stock page, type **264646449** into the search field and press Return/Enter.

7 This is the ID number of a wine bottle model. Click the License For Free button. The asset will be licensed, and downloaded to your browser's download location.

8 In Dimension, choose File > Import > 3D Model.

9 Navigate to your browser's default download location, open the folder named AdobeStock_182469425, select the file named a_wine_glass_1_125.obj, and click Open. The model will be placed in the center of the scene, positioned on the ground plane.

10 The wine glass is quite small compared to the background image. To enlarge the glass proportionally, click the open lock icon next to Size in the Properties panel. Then enter **10 cm** for the X value.

Size ∨ 🔒

X 10 cm   Y 21.59 cm   Z 10 cm

11 Choose File > Import > 3D Model.

12 Navigate to your browser's default download location, open the folder named AdobeStock_264646449, select the file named packaging_wine_bottle.obj, and click Open. The model will be placed in the center of the scene, positioned on the ground plane.

13 To make the bottle larger, click the open lock icon next to Size in the Properties panel. Then enter **9 cm** for the X value.

14 Use the Select tool (keyboard shortcut: V) to size and position the wine bottle and wine glass on the wood tabletop as desired. Since the wine glass is clear, it

Tip: Each time you press the \ (back slash) key, Preview mode will be toggled on or off.

will only display accurately if you have Render Preview turned on. I recommend that you work with Render Preview turned on for the rest of this lesson.

15 Hold down the Option key (macOS) or Alt key (Windows), and drag out a duplicate of the wine glass. As long as you drag only the red or blue arrows, the glass will remain on the ground plane (aligned with the wood in our scene) as you move it.

16 Repeat step 14 three more times, positioning the resulting five glasses as you want them to appear.

17 You may need to select the Orbit tool (keyboard shortcut: 1) and rotate your view of the scene temporarily so that you can see how the objects are positioned relative to each other. When you are finished, choose Camera > Switch To Home View to return to the camera bookmark you saved earlier.

▶ **Tip:** Command+B (macOS) or Ctrl+B (Windows) is the keyboard shortcut for the Camera > Switch To Home View command. This is a frequently-used command that is worth learning.

Remember that your view of the background image doesn't transform with the camera tools. It's static. The camera tools transform only your view of the 3D models in the scene.

Using Drop To Ground

Dimension offers two methods for automatically positioning models on the ground plane. In this lesson you'll learn the difference between the two.

1   Move one of the wine glasses in the scene to the side, apart from the others.

2   Drag the green arrow up to move the glass above the table.

3   Drag the blue circle to rotate the glass in the Z direction approximately **−50°**.

4   Choose Object > Move To Ground.

This doesn't look very real, does it? I challenge you to do this with a real wine glass!

5 Choose Edit > Undo Transform.

6 Choose Object > Drop To Ground.

That's better! The Object > Drop To Ground command uses a physics-based algorithm to try to figure out how an object will land on the ground plane. Sometimes this is an easier way to align an object with the ground plane than the Object > Move To Ground command.

I'll leave it up to you to add your own label artwork to the wine bottle.

Adding a background image to an existing scene

Sometimes you'll assemble a scene in Dimension with one or more models and then decide later to composite the scene with a background image. Let's try this.

1   In Dimension, choose File > Open.

2   Select the file Lesson_10_02_begin.dn and click Open.

This scene was created without a background image in mind. The camera view was changed many times during the composition to aid in placing the chairs, table, and soda cans accurately in the scene. Now you need to add a background image and realistically incorporate the table and chairs into the image.

▶ **Tip:** You can also drag a graphic file from the Finder (macOS), File Explorer (Windows), or Adobe Bridge and drop it onto the canvas to import a background image.

3   Choose File > Import > Image As Background.

4   Select the file Village_square.jpg and click Open.

The background image arrives centered on the Dimension file. But the aspect ratio of the image is different from that of the Dimension file. You want the Dimension canvas to match the aspect ratio of the background image, and you want to increase the pixel dimensions of the Dimension file.

5   With the Select tool (keyboard shortcut: V), click the gray area surrounding the canvas.

6   In the Actions panel, click the Match Background Aspect Ratio icon . This changes the dimensions of the Dimension file to match the aspect ratio of the image.

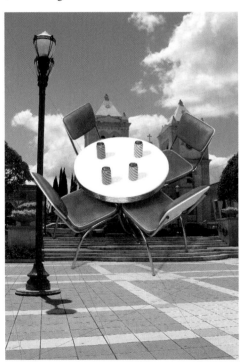

7 In the Properties panel, click the lock icon  next to Canvas Size to constrain the canvas proportions.

8 In the Width field, type ***3** after the 508 px text to multiply the width by 3 and then press Return/Enter.

Because you constrained the proportions by clicking the lock icon, the height is automatically calculated to keep the canvas proportional.

9 Choose View > Zoom To Fit Canvas.

Matching the scene to the image

If your background image contains strong perspective lines, as the image of the village square does, Dimension can attempt to match the camera perspective to the background image. This can save a lot of work fussing with the camera tools to get the perspective just right.

1 Click the background image on the canvas.

2 In the Properties panel, click the Match Image button.

3 Deselect the Resize Canvas To option, select Create Lights and Match Camera Perspective, select Outdoor Sunlight from the Create Lights menu, and then click OK.

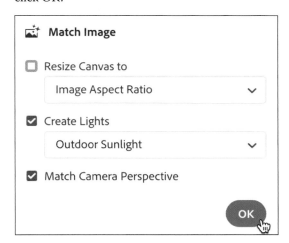

Note that the models are now aligned with the new perspective and camera angle, but that their relationship to each other stays the same.

4   To select all the models, choose Edit > Select All.

5   Drag the red and blue arrows to position the models as desired.

6   The direction and intensity of the shadows cast by the table and chairs matches the shadow cast by the street lamp. You can fine-tune the shadows by selecting Sun in the Scene panel and adjusting properties such as Intensity, Rotation, Height, and Cloudiness.

What to do when Match Image doesn't set the perspective correctly

In the first two exercises in this lesson, the Match Image command worked flawlessly, so creating the scene was easy. But sometimes Dimension isn't able to work out the perspective in the image and will need some help from you. This can happen for a variety of reasons. For example, the image might contain distortion that was introduced by a wide-angle lens or by image editing. Or sometimes an image won't have any visible vanishing lines from which Dimension can determine the perspective.

1 In Dimension, choose File > New.

2 Choose File > Import > Image As Background.

3 Select the file named Parking.jpg and click OK.

4 Select Environment in the Scene panel.

5 Choose Image > Match Image.

6 In the Match Image dialog box, select the Resize Canvas To option and select Image Size in the menu. Select Create Lights, and choose Outdoor Sunlight in the menu. Note that, in this case, the Match Camera Perspective option may be grayed out, indicating that Dimension can't extract enough information from the file to determine the perspective. If the Match Camera Perspective option is not grayed out, deselect the option so that you can learn what to do when Dimension is unable to help you with the perspective. Click the OK button.

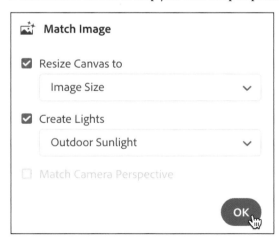

7 To begin to set the camera perspective manually, select the Horizon tool (keyboard shortcut: N).

8 Grab the horizon line at the top of the screen, and drag it down a bit. Aim for a location at approximately the place where the two parking stripes would meet if they were extended.

● **Note:** Because of the distortion introduced by some camera lenses, sometimes it is impossible to map the vanishing lines with exact precision. The key is to get close enough so that when you position your models in the scene, they look as if they belong there.

9 Right-click the Horizon tool, and select the Turn Camera tool.

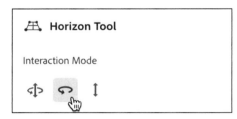

10 Click the image to dismiss the tool options box.

11 Drag across the image to the right repeatedly until the grid lines are vanishing toward the horizon in the middle of the screen.

12 Once you have the perspective the way you want it, save the camera location as a bookmark. Click the Camera Bookmarks icon at the top of the screen.

13 Click the plus icon ⊞ to create a new bookmark.

14 To rename the bookmark, type **Ending view** and press Enter/Return.

Adding a model to the scene

Once you've established a perspective in your scene that matches the background image, you can use this information to realistically position a model into the scene.

1 Click the Add And Import Content icon ⊕ at the top of the Tools panel.

2 Select Adobe Stock.

3 Select Browse All Adobe Stock 3D.

4 In your browser on the Adobe Stock page, type **201384101** into the search field and press Return/Enter.

5 Click the License For Free button. The asset will be licensed, and downloaded to your browser's download location.

6 In Dimension, choose File > Import > 3D Model.

7 Navigate to your browser's default download location, open the folder named AdobeStock_201384101, select the file named mini_pickup_truck_257.obj, and click Open.

8 The model arrives looking enormous compared to the background image, so all you see is a tiny portion of the model. To make the truck model better fit the scene, choose Camera > Frame Selection (keyboard shortcut: F).

9 With the Select tool (keyboard shortcut: V), drag the green circle to rotate the truck around the y-axis until it is facing forward.

10 In the Properties panel, click the lock icon 🔒 next to Size.

11 To make the truck larger, enter **350 cm** for the X value and press Return/Enter.

12 Use the Select And Move tool (keyboard shortcut: V) to position the truck as desired.

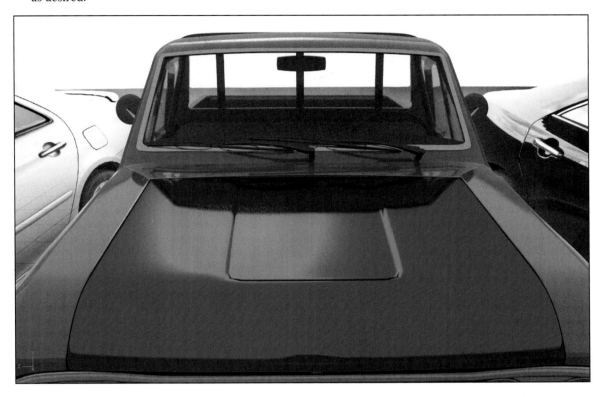

Building your own background

If you can't locate a suitable background image for your scene, you can either create a 2D background in a graphics program like Adobe Photoshop or Illustrator or construct a background using geometric models in Dimension.

Using a 2D background from Photoshop

Sometimes all you need to make your scene look realistic is a very simple background that can be easily constructed with a couple of colors or gradients in Photoshop.

1 In Dimension, choose File > Open.

2 Select the file Lesson_10_04_begin.dn and click Open.

3 Choose File > Import > Image As Background.

4   Select the file named Simple_background.psd and click Open.

This is just a simple image created in Photoshop with two different gradients that represent a "floor" and a "wall," or a "ground" and a "sky." You could of course create something much more complex using various colors, textures, and patterns.

5   Click the background image on the canvas to select the environment.

6   Choose Image > Match Image.

7   In the Match Image dialog, deselect the Resize Canvas To option, and select Create Lights. Note that, in this case, Dimension has chosen Abstract as the lighting type, since there isn't a strong light source in the image.

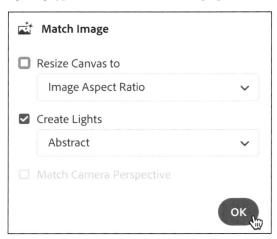

Dimension couldn't match the perspective for you because there are no perspective lines in this simple image, so the Match Camera Perspective option is grayed out. You'll need to position the horizon manually. Click OK.

8 Double-click or right-click the Horizon tool, and make sure the Turn And Raise/Lower Camera tool is selected.

9 Click away from the tool options box to dismiss it.

Note that no horizon line shows up on the canvas. This is due to the extreme camera angle in this case, causing the horizon to be way off the top of the canvas. This is indicated by the two off-screen icons ⬜ at the top left and top right of the document window.

10 Select the Orbit tool (keyboard shortcut: 1).

11 Drag up on the image until you are viewing the scene from the side.

12 Select the Horizon tool (keyboard shortcut: N).

13 Position the horizon line on the horizon line of the background image.

14 Click the Camera Bookmarks icon ⬚ at the top of the screen.

15 Click the plus icon ⊞ to create a new bookmark.

16 To rename the bookmark, type **Starting view** and press Enter/Return.

17 Use the Select, Pan, and Dolly tools to position the models in the scene as you see fit.

Building a 3D background in Dimension

Dimension includes some simple models—such as Curved Plane, Cloth Backdrop, Hollow Sphere, Hollow Cube, Plane, and Half Pipe—that you can use to construct a virtual "set" or "room" in which to pose your models. In this lesson you'll create two walls and a floor to display living room furniture.

1 In Dimension, choose File > New With Settings, and create a scene that is 3000 px x 2000 px.

2 Click the Add And Import Content icon 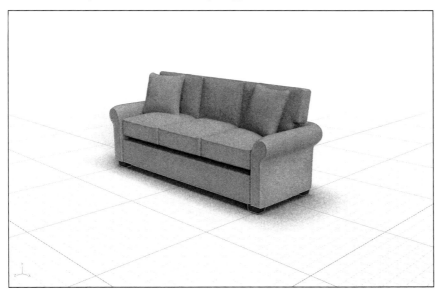 at the top of the Tools panel.

3 Select Adobe Stock.

4 Select Browse All Adobe Stock 3D.

5 In your browser on the Adobe Stock page, type **172868940** into the search field and press Return/Enter.

6 Click the License For Free button.

7 In Dimension, choose File > Import > 3D Model.

8 Navigate to your browser's default download location, open the folder named AdobeStock_172868940, select the file named a_couch_1_159.obj, and click Open.

9 Choose Camera > Frame All.

10 Select the Dolly tool (keyboard shortcut: 3) and drag down on the canvas to pull the camera away from the sofa, making it appear smaller.

11 Locate the Starter Asset named Plane, and place it in the scene. It will arrive small, positioned under the sofa, so you won't see it.

12 With the Plane model still selected, enter **500 cm** for both the X and Z values for Size in the Properties panel.

I like to import all or most of the models I'm going to use in a scene right at the beginning. This helps me see their sizes relative to each other. In this case, importing the sofa first helps you know how large the floor and walls need to be.

13 Double-click Plane in the Scene panel, and type **Floor** for the name of the model.

14 Choose Edit > Duplicate to create a copy of the Floor model.

15 In the Properties panel, enter **90°** for the X Rotation value. This will create the wall that will be positioned on the right.

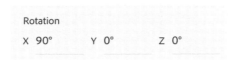

16 Double-click the Floor model that was just added to the Scene panel, and type **Right wall** for the name of the model.

17 Use the Select tool (keyboard shortcut: V) to drag the wall to the right so it's positioned near the right edge of the floor.

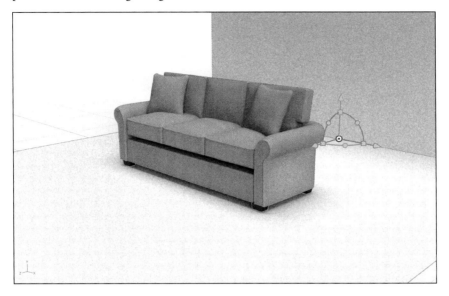

18 Select the Floor model again.

19 Choose Edit > Duplicate to create another copy of the floor.

20 In the Properties panel, enter **90°** for the Z Rotation value. This will create the wall that will be positioned on the left.

21 Double-click the Floor model that was just added to the Scene panel, and type **Left wall** for the name of the model.

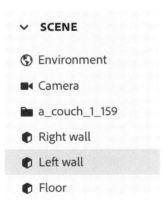

22 Drag the plane so it is positioned near the back of the "floor" plane.

It doesn't matter for our purposes that the wall planes intersect the ground plane and appear partially below the ground plane. You can only see what is above the ground plane anyway.

23 Select the Floor model.

24 Locate the Wood Parquet SBSAR model in the Starter Assets, and apply it to the Floor model.

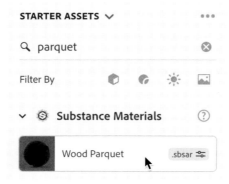

25 Experiment with the Wood Parquet material properties in the Properties panel until the floor looks the way you like.

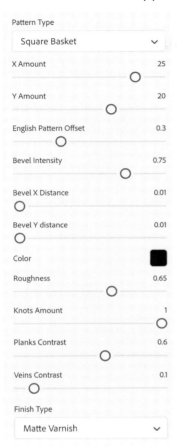

26 Double-click the Left wall model to reveal the model properties.

27 Click the color swatch next to base color, and select a color for the wall.

28 Double-click the Right wall model to reveal the model properties.

29 Click the color swatch next to base color, and select a color for the wall.

30 Position the sofa as desired.

31 Position the camera as desired.

Review questions

1 What are two ways to import a background image into a scene?

2 What are the three things that the Match Image feature attempts to do?

3 If the Match Image feature doesn't determine the perspective accurately, what tool would you use to begin correcting the perspective?

4 What are two ways to access the Match Image command?

Review answers

1 You can import a background image into a scene by choosing File > Import > Image As Background or by dragging and dropping an image onto the canvas from the macOS Finder, Windows File Explorer, or Adobe Bridge.

2 The Match Image feature allows you to resize the canvas to match the image size or aspect ratio, extract lighting information from the image and construct scene lighting to match, and match the perspective of the image.

3 The Horizon tool is the primary tool you would use to correct or tweak perspective.

4 Match Image can be found in Image > Match Image, as well as in the Actions panel when a background image is selected.

11

WORKING WITH LIGHTS

Lesson overview

In this lesson, you'll explore and apply lights in a 3D scene and learn the following:

- The difference between environment light and directional lights.
- How to automatically create environment light from a background image.
- How to change the properties of the sun light.
- How to load a new environment light and change its properties.
- How to work with multiple directional lights in a scene.

 This lesson will take about 45 minutes to complete. To get the lesson files used in this chapter, download them from the web page for this book at www.adobepress.com/DimensionCIB2020. For more information, see "Accessing the lesson files and Web Edition" in the Getting Started section at the beginning of this book.

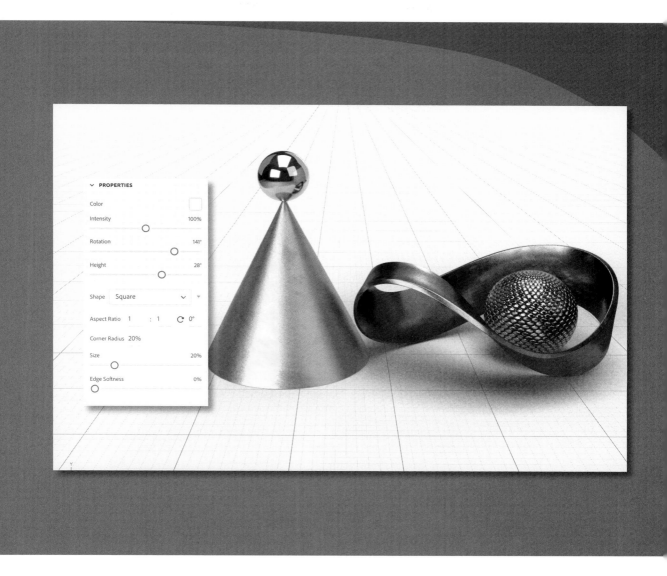

The rich set of lighting properties in Dimension allow you to create realistic looking highlights, shadows, and reflections.

Exploring three types of lights

Dimension files can contain three types of lighting: environment light, directional lights, and glowing materials. Environment lights are 360° images that offer great reflections and lighting and are useful for preset lighting setups. Multiple directional lights can be combined to create custom lighting that originates from multiple sources. Sun light is a special type of directional light that mimics sunlight and provides strong directional lighting and shadows. And some materials can contain a Glow property that will light up not only the model with the material applied but also adjacent surfaces. A scene may contain only environment light, only directional lights, only sun light, only glowing objects, or several types of lights at once.

Lighting that you add to your scene appears in the Scene panel under Environment. The attributes of the different types of lighting are controlled by settings in the Properties panel.

Experimenting with environment light

In this exercise, you'll experiment with the environment light in a partially completed scene and observe the results.

1   In Dimension, choose File > Open.

2   Select the file named Lesson_11_01_begin.dn, which is in the Lessons > Lesson11 folder that you copied onto your hard disk, and then click Open.

    To simulate what the plaza background image would look like with a modern sculpture added to it, I've placed the Mobius Strip model from the starter assets into the scene and applied the Metal material to the model surface. I've also matched the camera perspective to the model and saved it as a camera bookmark. But I haven't yet done anything with the lighting.

3   So that you can see accurate lighting, you'll want to click the Render Preview icon ![icon] if you don't already have Render Preview turned on. Remember, unless you have Render Preview turned on, you won't see any reflections, and will see only rough lighting and shadows.

4   In the Scene panel, select Environment to reveal Environment Light underneath if it isn't already visible, and then select Environment Light.

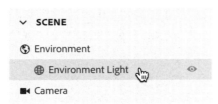

5 Hover over Environment Light and click the eye icon  to turn off the environment light. You'll see the model go completely dark, and see that it casts no shadows, because there is no environment light or other light source hitting the model surface.

6 Click the eye icon next to Environment Light again to turn the environment light back on. You'll see that there are highlights and reflections on the metallic surface of the model, but they don't seem to relate to the background image in any way.

7　In the Properties panel, click the image swatch next to Image.

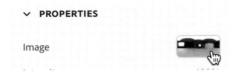

This displays the graphic being used for the environment light, which is currently the default environment light that is used automatically if no other environment light is specified. This default light simulates a typical studio lighting setup.

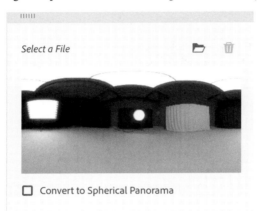

This scene would look much more realistic if the light hitting the model matched the light hitting the walls of the building, and if the plaza and building were reflected on the shiny surface of the model. Dimension can automatically extract this information from the background image for you.

8　Click on the background image on the canvas to select the environment.

9　In the Actions panel, click the Match Image button.

10 Select only the Create Lights option, choose Outdoor Sunlight from the Create Lights menu, and click OK.

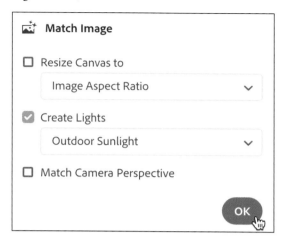

You'll see that the metallic surface now reflects the pattern on the concrete and the arches on the building.

11 Note also that the mobius strip is now casting strong shadows on the ground. This is because the Match Image command added a sun light source. In the Scene panel, hover over Sun and click the eye icon 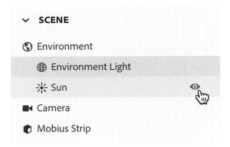 to hide the Sun light.

12 Select Environment Light again in the Scene panel if it isn't already selected.

13 In the Properties panel, click the image swatch next to Image.

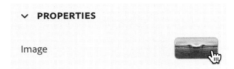

This displays a flat representation of the spherical image that Dimension automatically created from the background image.

14 Click the image swatch again to close the image picker.

15 In the Properties panel, increase Intensity to **130%**. This makes the overall lighting brighter, which will affect the models in the scene but not the background image.

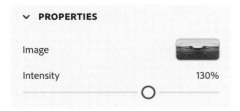

16 In the Properties panel, experiment with the Rotation slider. This rotates the spherical projection of the environment light, providing different reflections, highlights, and shadows on the model's surface.

17 In the Properties panel, click the white color swatch next to Colorize. Click the color sampler icon [icon] in the color picker, and click somewhere in the light blue area of the sky. You'll see the environment light take on a blue cast.

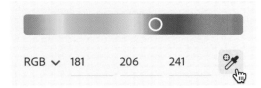

Using a bitmap image for the environment light

You can use any AI, EXR, HDRI, JPEG, PNG, PSD, SVG, or TIFF image as an environment light. When you do so, Dimension converts the image into a 360° panorama image, using Content Aware Fill technology to fill in the missing areas in the panorama.

1 In the Properties panel, deselect the Colorize option.

2 Choose File > Import > Image As Light.

3 Select the file named Clouds.jpg, and click Open.

► **Tip:** You'll get the best results using HDRI or EXR images for environment lights since they are high dynamic range and provide more lighting information than other image types.

4 In the Properties panel, click the image thumbnail next to Image to see the spherical image that Dimension produced from the JPEG image.

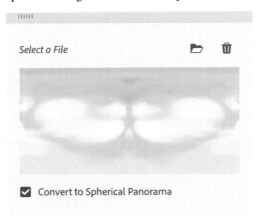

5 In the Scene panel, click the eye icon next to Sun to show the Sun light, adding the strong cast shadows to the scene once again.

Lights and file formats

When you use an AI, JPEG, PNG, PSD, SVG, or TIFF image as an environment light, dramatic lighting and shadows are not produced, since the images are low dynamic range and thus provide only ambient lighting and reflections. You can add dramatic lighting and shadows with sun light.

An HDRI or EXR image can be imported as an environment light. These high dynamic range images produce ambient lighting, reflections, and dramatic lighting and shadows.

You can also import an IBL (Image Based Light) file as an environment light. IBL files are packaged containers that hold multiple images for lighting, reflections, and backgrounds in a single package. This format produces very realistic-looking lighting, but due to inconsistencies in the file format, some IBL files that you find on the web will import and some will not.

Using starter asset environment lights

Applying lights to spheres and cones is helpful in understanding how certain types of lighting behave in Dimension, so in this exercise you'll apply and edit environment lights to a simple scene containing these objects.

1 Choose File > Open.

2 Select the file named Lesson_11_02_begin.dn, which is in the Lessons > Lesson11 folder that you copied onto your hard disk, and then click Open.

This file contains only the default environment light that is applied to every new file.

3　Click the Add And Import Content icon ⊕ at the top of the Tools panel.

4　Select Starter Assets.

5　Select the Lights icon ☀ to filter the assets to display only lights.

6　Select the Studio Warm Key Light.

▶ **Tip:** Hundreds of additional image-based environment lights, optimized specifically for use in Dimension, are available for purchase on Adobe Stock at stock.adobe.com.

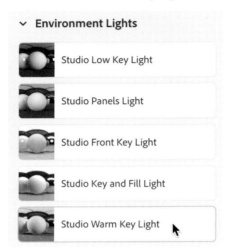

Note that the location of the highlights on the objects, the color of the light, and the direction of the shadows all change.

7   In the Scene panel, click Environment to reveal Environment Light underneath if it isn't already visible, and then select Environment Light.

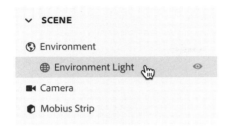

8   In the Properties panel, experiment with the Intensity, Rotation, and Colorize settings to see how these affect the Environment Light.

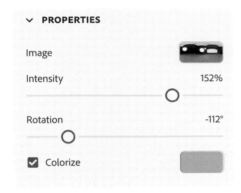

> **Note:** A scene can contain only a single Environment Light. In other words, only a single Environment Light will display in the Scene panel. This may be slightly confusing because the image used for an Environment Light can contain multiple lights within it.

9   In the Content panel, select the Studio Color Stage A environment light.

10 In the Properties panel, you'll see that the Intensity and Rotation values are set back to 100% and 0°, respectively, and the Colorize option is turned off. These values are reset every time that you apply a new environment light to your scene.

11 In the Properties panel, click the Image Picker next to Image. This will reveal the spherical panorama that is being used to generate the Studio Color Stage A lighting.

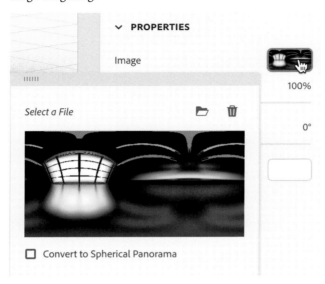

12 Select the Dolly tool (keyboard shortcut: 3), point at the Sphere model in the scene, and drag up to zoom in on the sphere. You'll see the reflections on the shiny metal surface of the sphere match the image displayed in the Image Picker.

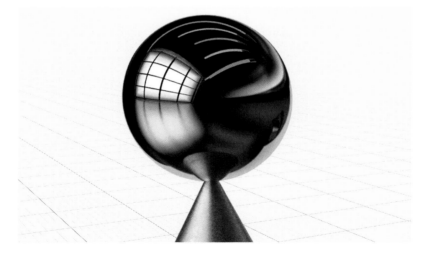

13 In the Properties panel, experiment with the Rotation slider; you'll see lighting reflections rotate around the surface of the Sphere model.

14 Choose Camera > Switch To Home View to reset the camera view.

Experimenting with sun light

In addition to environment light, a scene can also contain another light source called Sun, which is a special kind of directional light.

1 In the Content panel, select Sun under Directional Lights.

This creates strong directional shadows in the same direction as the much subtler shadows that were created by the environment light.

2 In the Scene panel, select Environment (not Environment Light)

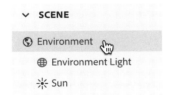

3 Experiment with the Global Intensity and Global Rotation values. These settings affect the intensity and rotation of all the lights in the scene—in this case your environment light and sun light.

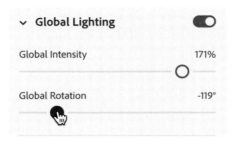

4 Choose Edit > Undo as many times as necessary until Global Intensity is set back to 100% and Global Rotation is set back to 0°.

5 In the Scene panel, select Sun.

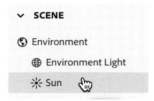

6 In the Properties panel, change the Rotation value to **100°**. This will cause the Sun to appear to be shining from somewhere above your right shoulder. You'll see the direction of the shadows change, and a new highlight appear on the front of the cone. The location of the highlights and shadows generated by the environment light, however, does not change.

● **Note:** The Intensity property controls the brightness of the light generated by the sun. Dimension automatically makes the sun brighter when it's high and dimmer when it's near the horizon.

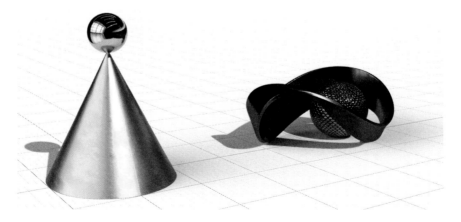

7 Change the Intensity value to 80%.

8　Change the Height value to **20°**. This will lower the sun to be located 20° above the horizon, making the cast shadows appear longer.

The Height property controls the vertical rotation of the sun. The sun remains shining from the same "direction," but the height in the sky changes. A value near 0° provides a very low light angle, producing long shadows. A value of 90° provides top-down lighting, as you would observe at noon, producing very short shadows.

9　Change the Cloudiness value to 40%. The Cloudiness property affects the "softness" of the cast shadows as well as the darkness. A cloudiness value of 0% creates shadows with hard edges, while a cloudiness value of 100% creates shadows with soft edges. The edges will appear softer the farther they are away from the model.

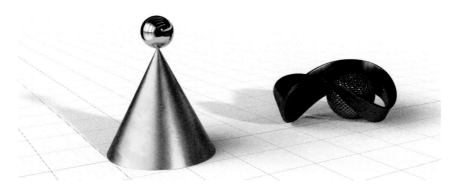

Note: In addition to changing the length of the shadows, the Height slider also changes the color of the light produced by the sun. A low sun angle produces reddish lighting, as you might find at dawn or dusk, while a value near 90° produces a bright white light, as you'd typically find near noon. This automatic coloring is overridden if the Colorize option is selected, which lets you choose your own color value for the sun light.

Experimenting with directional lights

Each scene can have only a single environment light and a single sun light. But you can add as many other directional lights to your scene as you wish.

1 Hover over Environment Light in the Scene panel and click the eye icon 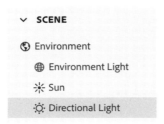 to hide the environment light.

2 In the same manner, hover over Sun and click the eye icon to hide the sun light.

3 In the Content panel, select Circle Light (one of the lights under Directional Lights). The light will appear in the Scene panel named Directional Light.

I added the metallic sphere to this scene to help you visualize the lights. Since you hid all the lighting except this single directional light, you can see the light source reflected in the sphere.

4   In the Properties panel, change the Size to **50%**, and the Edge Softness to **80%**. You'll see the reflection of the light change in the sphere.

5   Change the shape from Circle to Square.

6   Instead of changing the Rotation and Height values in the Properties panel, you can adjust these values another way. Select the Aim Light At Point icon ⊕ in the Actions panel.

7   Drag around on the surface of one of the models in the scene to direct the light to shine on that surface. This will change the Rotation and Height values as you drag.

8   Add a second and a third Circle Light or Square Light to your scene and position them as you wish. Note that each arrives in the Scene panel with the name Directional Light 2, Directional Light 3, etc. It is good practice to rename these (by purpose or direction or whatever works for you) so that you know which light is which in your scene.

9   Remove the three directional lights from your scene (select each in the Scene panel and click the trash icon 🗑 in the Actions panel).

10 In the Content panel under Directional Lights, select 3-Point Light. This adds three lights to the Scene panel: a Key Light, a Fill Light, and a Back Light. These are three square directional lights pre-configured in the traditional three-point light setup commonly used by studio photographers. Each of these lights can be modified in the Properties panel like any other directional light.

Experimenting with glow

A scene may contain one other source of light: materials that glow. The material called Glowing (in the starter assets) is an example of such a material. This material creates its own light, unlike most of the other starter asset materials, which only reflect light by default.

1 Use the eye icons 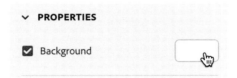 in the Scene panel to hide any lights that are in the scene, including the Environment Light, Sun, and Directional Lights. The models in the scene will become entirely black.

You might wonder why the background is still a light yellow when there is no more light being cast on the scene. This is because the background, whether it's a solid color or an image, is never affected by the lighting in the scene. This is easy to forget when you see realistic shadows cast on the background. But the brightness of the background never changes with the scene lighting. You will need to adjust that manually, either by changing the background color or editing the background image.

2 Click somewhere on the background with the Select tool to select the environment.

3 In the Properties panel, click the color swatch next to Background to edit the background color.

4 Enter values of **150** red, **150** green, and **150** blue and then click away from the color picker to make the background color a dark grey.

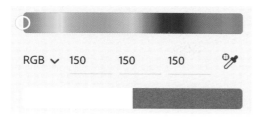

5 Also in the Properties panel, enter **10%** for the Reflection Opacity and **50%** for the Reflection Roughness.

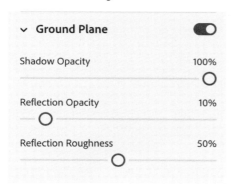

● **Note:** The light emitted by a model containing a material with the Glow property will have different effects on the ground plane based on the Ground Plane Reflection Opacity.

6 Click the Camera Bookmarks icon 🎬 and select the Mobius strip bookmark to reposition the camera on the Mobius strip model.

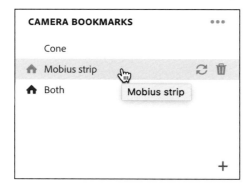

7 In the Scene panel, select the Sphere 2 model.

▶ Tip: You can make any of the MDL materials found in the starter assets "glow," or emit light, by adjusting the material's Glow value in the Properties panel.

8 In the Assets panel, select the Glowing material to apply it to the Sphere 2 model.

The Mobius strip model is now lit up by the light being emitted from the glowing material on the Sphere 2 model.

Review questions

1 What are three sources of light that can exist in a Dimension file?

2 What happens if a scene has no lights applied to it?

3 What effect does the Cloudiness property have on a scene?

4 What effect does increasing the height of the sun light have on a scene?

5 What file formats can be used for creating custom environment lights?

Review answers

1 Three sources of light are environment light, directional lights, (including sun light), and a material with the Glow property.

2 Models in the scene become almost completely black except for light reflected from the background. The background lighting does not change.

3 Increasing the Cloudiness property makes cast shadows lighter and softens the edges of the shadows.

4 As you increase the angle of the sun light, shadows grow shorter, and the color of the sun light becomes more white.

5 Files in the following formats can be used to create custom Environment Light: AI, EXR, HDRI, JPEG, PNG, PSD, SVG, or TIFF. EXR and HDRI images will provide the best results due to their high dynamic range.

12 EXPORTING MODELS AND SCENES

Lesson overview

In this lesson, you'll discover how to export models and scenes from Dimension, and learn the following:

- How to save a selected model for reuse in another scene.

- How Dimension works with Creative Cloud Libraries.

- How to export a scene for viewing on the web.

- How to export a model for use in augmented reality workflows.

This lesson will take about 45 minutes to complete. To get the lesson files used in this chapter, download them from the web page for this book at www.adobepress.com/DimensionCIB2020. For more information, see "Accessing the lesson files and Web Edition" in the Getting Started section at the beginning of this book.

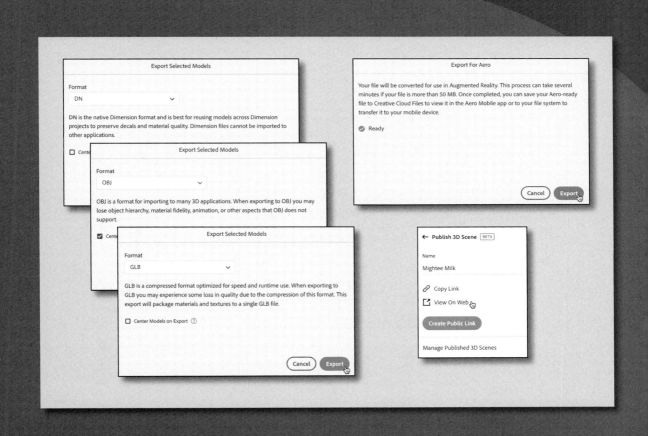

Dimension includes robust export capabilities that
let you export models for use in other Dimension
scenes or other 3D programs, for viewing on the web,
or for use in augmented reality programs such as
Adobe Aero.

Exporting models and scenes

The primary purpose of Dimension is to help you create 3D scenes by importing 3D models from a variety of sources, applying materials and graphics to the surfaces of the models, and arranging the models into a scene, complete with custom lighting and background images. As you've learned, you can save these scenes with File > Save. Scenes are saved into Dimension's proprietary DN file format, which can only be opened by Dimension.

But Dimension also lets you export selected models to the DN format, and export selected models or entire scenes to other formats. This can be useful for exporting individual models to Dimension format without the scene information, or for exporting models or entire scenes to be used by other programs.

Dimension can export content to the following file formats:

DN This is Dimension's proprietary file format. Export to this format to share a model with another Dimension user, or to use a model in a different scene.

glTF GL Transmission Format, a "royalty-free specification for the efficient transmission and loading of 3D scenes and models by applications". For more information, see www.khronos.org/gltf.

GLB The binary version of the glTF format.

OBJ Wavefront OBJ Format, a common 3D file format standard supported by many 3D modeling programs.

Exporting a model to DN format

Exporting a model to the proprietary Dimension DN file format is the best choice if you are going to re-use the model in another Dimension scene. This file format will reliably save the materials and graphics applied to the model.

When you export a model, you have the option to reset the coordinates so that the model will be placed into the center of any scene into which it's imported, much like most starter assets. You can also choose to save the original coordinates with the model. In this lesson you'll see how this works.

1   Open the file named Lesson_12_01_begin.dn, which is in the Lessons > Lesson12 folder that you copied onto your hard disk. Be patient. This is a large file that may open slowly.

2 Use the Select tool to select the leftmost skim milk bottle in the front row.

3 Look in the Properties panel under Position, and make note of the coordinates of the bottle: x=19.7 cm, y=1 cm, z=37.3 cm.

4 Choose File > Export > Selected Models.

5 Choose DN for the Format.

6 Do not select the Center Models On Export option.

7 Click the Export button.

8 Type **Skim milk not centered.dn** for the filename, choose a location where you can find the file again later in this lesson, and click Save.

9 Once again, choose File > Export > Selected Models.

10 Choose DN for the Format.

11 This time, select the Center Models On Export option.

12 Click the Export button.

▶ **Tip:** The easy-to-remember keyboard shortcut to export selected models is Command+E (macOS) and Ctrl+E (Windows).

13 Type **Skim milk centered.dn** for the filename, choose a location where you can find the file again later in this lesson, and click Save.

14 Choose File > New With Settings, and create a new document that is **1024 px** wide and **768 px** high. Dimension will close the Lesson_12_begin.dn file, and create a new file. (If you are prompted to save the file that is being closed, you can click Don't Save.)

15 Choose File > Import > 3D Model.

16 Select the Skim milk not centered.dn model, and click Open.

17 The bottle will be imported, but only a small part of the bottle will be visible.

In the Properties panel under Position you'll see that the bottle indeed landed in the correct coordinates (x=19.7 cm, y=1 cm, z=37.3 cm).

The reason that the position of the bottle appears different in this new file is that the camera is oriented toward the scene differently than in the original file.

18 Choose File > Import > 3D Model.

19 Select the Skim milk centered.dn model, and click Open. This file will import exactly in the center of the scene, as expected.

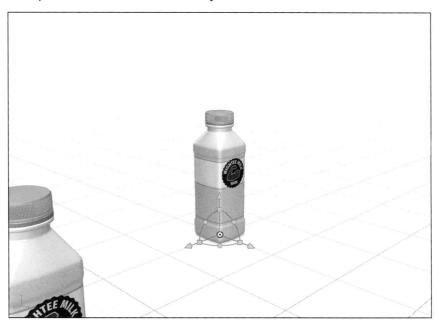

Exporting a model to GLB format

As mentioned earlier, glTF and GLB are closely related. GLB is simply the binary, single-file version of the glTF format. The creator of this format calls it the "jpeg of 3D formats". The format is supported by a wide variety of software programs and web services. In this exercise, you'll export both a model and an entire scene, and place the results in a PowerPoint presentation.

1 Open the file named Lesson_12_01_begin.dn, which is in the Lessons > Lesson12 folder that you copied onto your hard disk. Dimension will close the file with the two skim milk bottles. (When you are prompted to save the file that is being closed, you can click Don't Save.)

2 Use the Select tool to select the bottle on the far right (the front red whole milk bottle).

3 Choose File > Export > Selected Models.

4 Choose GLB for the format.

5 Select the Center Models On Export option.

6 Click the Export button.

7 Type **Whole milk bottle.glb** for the filename, choose a location where you can find the file again later in this lesson, and click Save.

8 Choose File > Export > Scene.

9 Choose GLB for the Format.

10 Click the Export button.

11 Type **Milk bottle scene.glb** for the filename, choose a location where you can find the file again later in this lesson, and click Save.

12 If you have access to Microsoft PowerPoint, open the file named Presentation.ppx, which is in the Lessons > Lesson12 folder that you copied onto your hard disk.

● **Note:** 3D models can be inserted into Microsoft PowerPoint, Word, Excel, and Outlook. However, depending on your particular Microsoft Office license and the version of your operating system, this feature may not be available.

13 In PowerPoint, choose Insert > 3D Models > From A File.

14 Select the Whole milk bottle.glb file that you exported earlier, and click Insert.

15 Drag around on the rotation widget to position the bottle as desired.

16 Press the delete key to delete the model.

17 Choose Insert > 3D Models > From A File.

18 Select the Milk bottle scene.glb file that you exported earlier, and click Insert.

19 Drag around on the rotation widget to position the bottle as desired.

20 Click on Animations to reveal the Animations ribbon.

21 Select the Turntable animation. You should see the milk bottle scene begin to rotate 360°.

Exporting a model to OBJ format

If you need to export a model for use in a 3D software program that doesn't support the glTF or GLB forms, it's likely that you can use the OBJ format.

1 In Dimension, use the Select tool to select one of the blue 2 percent milk bottles.

2 Choose File > Export > Selected Models.

3 Choose OBJ for the format.

4 Select the Center Models On Export option.

5 Click the Export button.

6 Type **Two percent milk bottle.obj** for the filename, choose a location where you will be able to find the file, and click Save.

7 In the Macintosh Finder or Windows File Explorer, examine the location where you exported the OBJ file. Note that a Two percent milk bottle.obj file and a Two percent milk bottle.mtl file were both exported, along with a folder named "Two percent milk bottle" that contains some PNG files. Both files and the folder are necessary to successfully import the OBJ file into another 3D program.

Saving model assets in a Creative Cloud Library

CC Libraries are a great way to save and store design assets and then reuse those assets across projects and between Creative Cloud programs. Dimension supports storing models, colors, and graphics in Libraries, and allows you to retrieve models, colors, and graphics from Libraries and use them in your scenes.

1 Click the Add And Import Content icon ⊕ at the top of the Tools panel, and choose CC Libraries. This displays the Content panel on the left side of the screen, and shows the last-used CC Library in the panel.

2 At the top of the panel, click the more icon ••• and choose Create New Library.

3 Type **Mightee Milk** for the library name, and click Create.

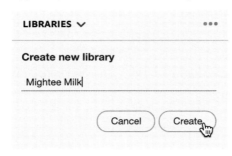

► **Tip:** You can have as many different Creative Cloud libraries as you wish. You may wish to organize your libraries by project, asset type, client, or any criteria that makes sense in your workflow.

4 Use the Select tool to select one of the green skim milk bottles.

5 Click the plus icon ⊞ at the bottom of the CC Libraries panel.

6 Choose Model from the menu. The skim milk bottle will be added to the Mightee Milk library.

7 Use the Select tool to select one of the blue 2 percent milk bottles.

8 Click the plus icon ⊞ at the bottom of the CC Libraries panel.

9 Choose Model from the menu. The 2 percent milk bottle will be added to the Mightee Milk library.

10 Double-click one of the blue bottle caps on a 2 percent milk bottle to reveal the material applied to the cap.

11 In the Properties panel, click the blue color swatch next to Base Color.

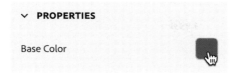

12 To add the blue color to the Mightee Milk library, click the Add To CC Libraries icon ![icon] in the color picker.

13 Choose Edit > Deselect All

14 Double-click one of the Mightee Milk labels on a 2 percent milk bottle to select the label graphic.

15 In the Properties panel, click the image swatch next to Image.

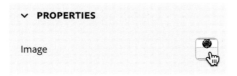

16 To add the label image to the Mightee Milk library, click the Add To CC Libraries icon ![icon] in the image picker.

17 Your Mightee Milk library should now contain two models, one graphic, and one color. These assets can now be used in any other Dimension projects you work on. The graphic and color can also be used in other Creative Cloud programs

such as Illustrator, Photoshop, and InDesign. You may want to right-click on each asset in the library and choose rename to give the assets meaningful names to make them easier to identify later.

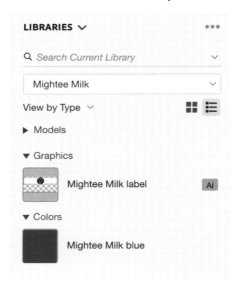

Exporting a scene to the Web

Dimension includes a way for you to share your scene with others through an automatically-generated Web link, allowing them to interact with your scene in 3D space.

1   Open the file named Lesson_12_02_begin.dn, which is in the Lessons > Lesson12 folder that you copied onto your hard disk. (If you are prompted to save a file that is being closed, you can click Don't Save.)

2   Click the Camera Bookmarks icon ![icon]. Note that this file contains four clearly named bookmarks.

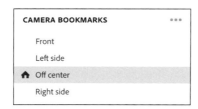

3   Click the Share icon 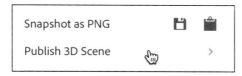 in the upper-right corner of the screen.

4   Select Publish 3D Scene.

5   Type a name, and click Create Public Link.

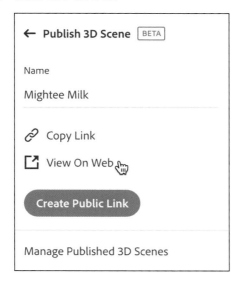

6   Click View on Web.

7   In your web browser, experiment with viewing the scene from different angles, zoom in and out, and try some of the other features. Click the help icon ⓘ to learn how to manipulate the scene in 3D space with a mouse or trackpad (the shortcuts are different from those used in Dimension).

Note that each camera bookmark from the scene in Dimension displays as an icon in the browser that provides quick access to that view.

Exporting for augmented reality workflows

Adobe Aero is a new augmented reality authoring tool to help designers create "immersive content." It allows designers to pose 3D models in a physical space, and apply behaviors to the models so that they respond to touch and other commands. Models from Dimension can be exported for use in Aero.

1   Open the file named Lesson_12_03_begin.dn, which is in the Lessons > Lesson12 folder that you copied onto your hard disk. (If you are prompted to save a file that is being closed, you can click Don't Save.)

2   Use the Select tool to select the Astronaut model.

3   Choose File > Export > Selected For Aero.

4   After a brief pause, Dimension will indicate that the model is ready for export. Click the Export button.

Note: The astronaut model is from the repository of free 3D models available from NASA at nasa3d.arc.nasa.gov/models.

5   Navigate to the Creative Cloud Files folder on your computer, type **Astronaut** for the filename, and click Save. Saving the file into your Creative Cloud Files folder will make it easy to import the model into Aero on your mobile device, since Aero has access to these files.

6   Download the Adobe Aero app from www.adobe.com/products/aero.html and install it on your mobile device.

7   Launch the Aero app on your mobile device.

8   Tap the plus icon ⊕ to start a new project.

9   Slowly pan the device camera around physical surface on which you wish to pose the astronaut model.

10 When the surface is located, tap the pin to create an anchor for the model.

11 Tap the plus icon ⊕ and then choose Creative Cloud.

12 Select the Astronaut model that you saved into your Creative Cloud Files folder earlier.

13 Tap Open. The model will be imported into the scene.

14 Tap Preview to preview the result.

There's a lot more that you can do with Aero. This is just a quick look at how to bring a model from Dimension into Aero.

Review questions

1   What are four file formats that Dimension can use for model export?

2   Why would you want to export a single model from a scene in the Dimension format?

3   What file format would you use to export a model for use in Microsoft Office?

4   Which three types of assets from Dimension can be saved in a Creative Cloud Library?

5   Why is it helpful to save several different views of a scene as Camera Bookmarks before using the Publish 3D Scene command?

Review answers

1   Dimension can export models in the DN, gLTF, GLB, and OBJ file formats.

2   The DN file format is the most robust export format to use if you are going to use the model in another scene.

3   The GLB format works well for importing 3D models into Microsoft Office applications such as Word, PowerPoint, and Excel.

4   Models, graphics, and colors from Dimension scenes can all be saved into a CC Library.

5   Any saved Camera Bookmarks in a scene are turned into saved "views" that the user can click in a Web browser to view the scene from that camera angle.

13 POST-PROCESSING WITH ADOBE PHOTOSHOP

Lesson overview

In this lesson, you'll discover why and how you would open in Adobe Photoshop a scene that was rendered by Dimension, and you'll learn the following:

- Which Photoshop layers are created automatically by Dimension's renderer and what you can use them for.

- How to easily change the background image in Photoshop.

- How to use the masks that are automatically saved into the rendered image to make selections easier.

- How to apply simple color correction to a rendered scene in Photoshop.

This lesson will take about 45 minutes to complete. To get the lesson files used in this chapter, download them from the web page for this book at www.adobepress.com/DimensionCIB2020. For more information, see "Accessing the lesson files and Web Edition" in the Getting Started section at the beginning of this book.

When you render a scene to the PSD format,
Dimension adds several useful layers to the file that
make certain post-processing tasks easier.

Opening a scene rendered as a PSD file in Photoshop

Dimension is the easiest place in which to make changes to the lighting, color, background, and composition of your Dimension scenes. But occasionally you might need to edit a scene in Photoshop after it has been rendered. For example, you might want to make a quick tweak to the overall color of the scene without re-rendering the entire scene. Or you might need to work on the image after you've converted it to CMYK for print output in Photoshop. Or you might want to manipulate the image in some way that can be done only in Photoshop.

As you saw in an earlier lesson, Dimension can save the rendered output as a PNG file or as a PSD file. The main difference is that a PNG file is "flat." There are no layers, masks, or other helpful extras saved with a PNG file. However, if you save the rendered scene as a PSD file, Dimension adds extras to the file that make it easier to edit, or "post-process," the scene.

1   Launch Adobe Photoshop.

2   Choose File > Open.

3   Select the file named Lesson_13_begin_high_quality_render.psd, which is in the Lessons > Lesson13 folder that you copied onto your hard disk, and then click the Open button.

4   If your Layers panel isn't visible on the screen, choose Window > Layers.

    Your Layers panel should contain seven layers. Let's look at how you can use these layers.

Editing the background

Because the models are all rendered onto a transparent layer separate from the background, it is easy to make changes to the background behind the models.

Changing the background color

Changing the background color of the background is straightforward. Here's one way to do this in Photoshop.

1 Click the eye icon  next to the layer named Background Image to hide the layer.

2 Double-click the thumbnail icon on the Background Color layer to access the color picker.

3 Select a new color for the background, and click OK.

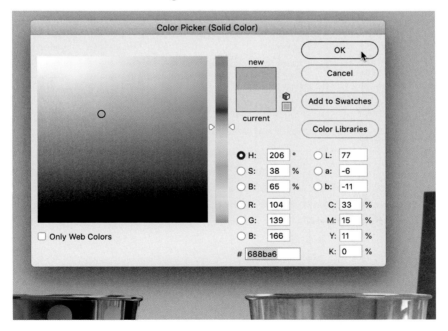

The shadows cast by the models on the background are semi-transparent, so they blend realistically with the new colored background. If this image had reflections that were reflecting on the ground plane, those reflections would also be retained and blend realistically with the new background color.

The water glass, however, still shows the background image in the glass. Semi-transparent materials are rendered with the background image in the material. This can make it difficult to edit scenes containing models with semi-transparent materials in Photoshop.

Changing the background image

Since the background image is rendered on its own Photoshop layer, it can easily be swapped out with a different image. However, your scene will not look very realistic unless the new background image has similar perspective and lighting as the original background image.

1   Click the eye icon ![eye icon] to the left of the Background Color layer to hide that layer.

Note that the 3D models are all rendered on a single layer named "Rendered Image (Reduced Noise)" and that the area around the models on this layer is a light gray checkerboard, indicating that it is transparent. Since this area is transparent, you can insert a new layer with a new background image beneath this layer to replace the background.

2   Choose File > Place Embedded.

3   Select the file named Checkerboard.jpg, which is in the Lessons > Lesson13 folder that you copied onto your hard disk, and then click Place.

4   Double-click the image to place it.

The image is placed on a new layer, named Checkerboard.

5   Drag the new layer beneath the layer named Background Image in the Layers panel.

The scene looks pretty good because the new background has a perspective similar to the old background. But the original image still appears when viewed through the glass, and the reflections that appear on the models are created from the original background. This would be very difficult to fix in Photoshop.

Modifying the background image

You've seen that replacing the background image can be problematic because of translucent objects and reflections on the surface of objects. But simple edits to the background image such as color correction, sharpening, and blurring can often be done without destroying the realism of the scene.

1 Click the eye icon ⊙ next to the Checkerboard layer in the Layers panel to hide the layer.

2 Click in the eye column next to Background Image in the Layers panel to reveal the original background.

3 Click Background Image in the Layers panel to select that layer.

4 Choose Layer > New Adjustment Layer > Brightness/Contrast.

5 Click OK in the New Layer dialog box. This creates a new Brightness/Contrast adjustment layer above the Background Image layer.

6   In the Properties panel, drag the Contrast slider all the way to the right to increase the contrast. This increases the contrast only in the Background Image layer, not in the layers above it.

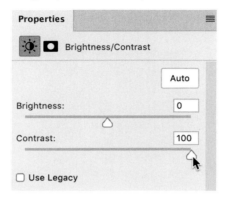

Using masks to make selections

When you render an image in the PSD format, Dimension creates a layer called Object Selection Masks, in which every 3D model in the scene is filled with a separate solid color on a black background. This layer makes it easy to select the outlines of each model in the rendering.

You'll use this layer to change the color of the spotted glass on the left side of the scene.

1   In the Layers panel, click the eye column next to Additional Layers to show the layer group.

2   Click the eye icon 👁 next to Material Selection Masks to hide that layer.

3   Select the Object Selection Masks layer.

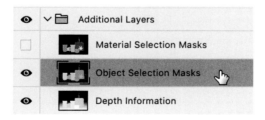

4   Select the Magic Wand tool (underneath the Object Selection tool and the Quick Selection tool in the Tools panel).

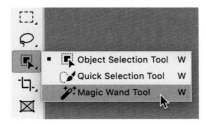

5   In the options bar, make sure that Tolerance is set to 0, that Anti-alias and Contiguous are selected, and that Sample All Layers is deselected.

Tolerance: 0   ✓ Anti-alias ✓ Contiguous ☐ Sample All Layers

6   On the Object Selection Masks layer, click the yellow color, which represents the left-most glass.

7   In the Layers panel, click the eye icon next to Additional Layers to hide that layer group.

8   Select the Rendered Image (Reduced Noise) layer in the Layers panel. Now the cup on that layer is precisely selected, based on the selection we made in the Object Selection Masks layer.

9   Select Layer > New > Layer Via Copy.

10 Double-click the layer name and change it to **Dotted cup**.

11 Choose Layer > Layer Style > Color Overlay.

12 Choose Color from the Blend Mode menu.

13 Click the color swatch, choose a blue color, and click OK.

14 Click OK again to close the Layer Style dialog box.

Adjusting materials

Dimension automatically creates a layer named Material Selection Masks in each rendered PSD file. This layer contains individual solid-color shapes that represent each material applied to the surface of a model. You'll use this layer to change the look of one of the materials used for the Star model.

1   Click the eye column next to the Additional Layers layer group to show the group.

2   Compare the filled area that represents the star on the Object Selection Masks layer to the filled area that represents the star on the Material Selection Masks layer by using the eye column to show and hide the layers.

You should see that the Object Selection Masks layer displays a single color for the entire Star model. But since two different materials are applied to the different facets of the Star model, the Material Selection Masks layer represents these two materials with two separate colors.

3   In the Layers panel, make sure the Material Selection Masks layer is visible, and click the layer to select it.

4   With the Magic Wand tool, click one of the light-colored facets of the Star model.

5   Choose Select > Similar to add all the light-colored facets of the Star model to the selection.

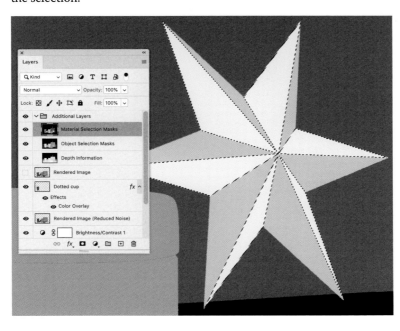

6   Click the eye icon next to the Additional Layers layer group to hide the group.

7   Select the Rendered Image (Reduced Noise) layer in the Layers panel.

8   Choose Filter > Pixelate > Pointillize.

9   Set Cell Size to **3**, and click OK.

▶ **Tip:** You can use the Depth Information layer as a mask to add depth of field effects or dramatic lighting to the scene. In the Depth Information layer, dark-colored areas are farther away from the camera, and lighter areas are closer to the camera.

Correcting color in the image

I want the overall color of the entire scene, including the background, to be a bit warmer. There are many ways to do this in Photoshop. Here's one way that doesn't require flattening the layers in the image.

1 Select the Rendered Image (Reduced Noise) layer in the Layers panel, and then Shift-click the Background Image layer.

2 Choose Layer > New > Group From Layers.

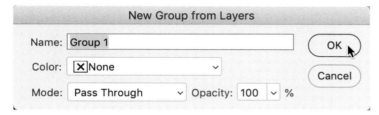

3 Click OK.

4 Choose Filter > Convert For Smart Filters.

5 Choose Filter > Camera Raw Filter.

6 Drag the Temperature slider to the right to make the image warmer.

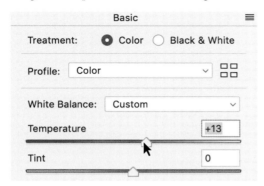

7 Click OK.

You can do much more to a 2D scene in Photoshop, of course. You are limited only by your imagination, your skill, and your knowledge of Photoshop.

Review questions

1   What is the advantage of saving a render from Dimension in the PSD format instead of in the PNG format?

2   What type of material could make it more difficult to realistically edit a background image in Photoshop?

3   Which layer contains a colored mask for each material applied to the surface of a model?

Review answers

1   The PSD format contains extra layers that make the image easier to edit. A scene rendered as a PNG will be a single-layer flat image.

2   Images that are semi-transparent, such as glass, once rendered, can make it difficult to swap in a new background in Photoshop.

3   The Material Selection Masks layer contains a separate colored mask for each part of a model that has a material applied to it.

INDEX

V

views
   cycling through, 62
   displaying in Scene panel, 83
   enlarging and reducing, 99
   resetting, 54

W

walls, creating, 237–242
Wavefront (OBJ) format, 93, 268
Web, exporting scenes to, 276–278
Web Edition, 3
websites, sources for 3D content, 99
Wood Parquet material, 241

X

x direction, moving objects in, 36
x-axis, 33, 163

Y

y direction, moving objects in, 36
y-axis, 33, 163

Z

z direction, moving objects in, 36
Z value for Rotation, 20, 23
z-axis, 163
zooming in and out, 12, 19

The fastest, easiest, most comprehensive way to learn
Adobe Creative Cloud

Classroom in a Book®, the best-selling series of hands-on software training books, helps you learn the features of Adobe software quickly and easily.

The **Classroom in a Book** series offers what no other book or training program does—an official training series from Adobe Systems, developed with the support of Adobe product experts.

To see a complete list of our Classroom in a Book titles covering the 2020 release of Adobe Creative Cloud go to:

www.adobepress.com/CC2020

Adobe Photoshop Classroom in a Book (2020 release)
ISBN: 9780136447993

Adobe Illustrator Classroom in a Book (2020 release)
ISBN: 9780136412670

Adobe InDesign Classroom in a Book (2020 release)
ISBN: 9780136502678

Adobe Dreamweaver Classroom in a Book (2020 release)
ISBN: 9780136412298

Adobe Premiere Pro Classroom in a Book (2020 release)
ISBN: 9780136602200

Adobe Dimension Classroom in a Book (2020 release)
ISBN: 9780136583936

Adobe XD Classroom in a Book (2020 release)
ISBN: 9780136583806

Adobe Audition CC Classroom in a Book, Second edition
ISBN: 9780135228326

Adobe After Effects Classroom in a Book (2020 release)
ISBN: 9780136411871

Adobe Animate Classroom in a Book (2020 release)
ISBN: 9780136449331

Adobe Photoshop Lightroom Classic Classroom in a Book (2020 release)
ISBN: 9780136623793

Adobe**Press**